AF544961

He Brings The Sun

April Jones Daugherty

Copyright © 2009 April Jones Daugherty
ISBN 978-0-9819376-3-2
All rights reserved.
Manufactured in the U.S.A.

Published by

You Lead

My tears have made me clean.
You've watched as I tried to keep them in.
But kept in my heart could only mean –
I'd have drowned in the rivers of where I've been.

I've learned the sun is Yours to bring,
and You've brought it every dawn, so I would know
after winter, You always deliver Spring.
... I've dreamt of fields where hearts not heavy, can
often go...

Now I hear my laughter. And You're with me.
You never left – but led me here where I could bloom.
No brighter could, such this perfect Son be:
Trusting You I'll stay – even if winter come again –
too soon.

Table of Contents

A Note from the Author

What is this book about? ...Well, in a word... Him. It's about Him. It's also about me, and cancer, and love, and pain, and fathers and daughters, and lessons, ... but at the heart of it, the unbroken line that runs through this book, is Him. This book is His story. I'm sure others will say this book is a memoir. They'll say it's my story. It will be shelved in the memoir section. It will be described as a coming of age story of a girl named April who lived through heartache and came out on the other side. But that will be a little shy of the truth. It's really His story; it always has been. Me? I'm simply blessed enough to be written in. I'm blessed enough to have been given His love first—followed by a journal, a computer, and finally a hunger to share all of it with you. Now my only request is that you turn the first page. That you dare to find Him within the lines; that you dare to encounter more than just another memoir. It's my prayer that you dare to encounter Love, and that you come away from the last page curious and pensive as you consider His story. Not His story as he wrote it across my life, but His story as it's written on the pages of your own.

April Jones Daugherty

PRELUDE: A GLIMPSE

H i m

Fall 2002

I could count the number of times I've been here. While it is *not* one of my favorite places, I know it is a part of me. Usually I prefer the distance I've made in the last four years to the encounter I always have with my past when I return. So you could say that I recall the details of each of my visits to this place—well, you could almost say that.

There was a season in my life when time after time I would seem to just end up here, and I would swear that my car had driven without me. I have friends who have since told me how they remember that winter and spring being filled with afternoons of driving by and seeing me standing in this very spot. Of course, I never saw them—not once.

Today was kind of like that. I was almost home, and then I saw the sign. It probably took half a second to decide I was turning. No, "decide" is not the right word, because it never feels like I decide. It is more like I realize, suddenly, that in this moment there is only one place I have to be; *need* to be.

So here I stand. I come here less and less, and this time I've been away longer than ever. Since that far away November, I've moved four times, but I guess I still have yet to leave.

Today it feels like there is more and also less to say. I never can just start. Not knowing what draws me, I spend the first few minutes silent and still. Like a movie that I once lived but now only watch, I stand here and let memories find their way back. Until this moment, it's always a mystery what I'll need to let my heart see this day. But one thing is consistent: the numbness that spreads back over my bones; that comfortable suit I wore for so long.

If I finally allow the numbness to break down, it's always an act of the will. Then I must gather up my heart and force those first words through the thickest silence. Sometimes words never come, and I retreat to my car. Like a waking dream, it's hard then to remember where I had been going, or what I had been planning to do, before I ended up here. But when the words do come, some of that emotional congestion I pretend not to feel finds relief. Every once in a while, a seldom tear will even make it all the way to the earth at my feet. These tears are so rare, especially in this genuine form, that I feel sure God takes the watered ground and grows something new from beneath it.

That has always been His promise to me. My name means 'new life,' and He has never failed to give me that. If not for His brand of love, I, like the one who lies beneath this simple grave, would have ceased to go on long ago. In the midst of those days and nights, when I thought that the pain would never release me, He was, in fact, the One who held me.

THE SWAY

Pretend

In my most grown-up voice, I call out, "Welcome back, Ted! Why don't you pick a chair, and then you can twist it around to look at any T.V. you want. I think the Forty-Niners are even playing on one of our many big screens. I have to finish getting everything ready, but can I get you a beer or some peanuts first?"

"A beer would be wonderful, Sally."

Grinning from ear to ear, my ten-year-old self darted toward the kitchen to fetch my "customer's" beverage of choice. This was going to be a perfect weekend of sports and charades! Why? Because we were playing my favorite game of pretend: "Sports Bar Barbershop."

As a coach's daughter with a vivid imagination, our game evolved naturally: 1) Dad loved football. 2) I loved playing beauty shop. 3) I had no siblings to play with. 4) Mom wouldn't let me 'fix' her hair. 5) Dad went sort-of comatose after opening kickoff. And 6) I had found a way to capitalize on the situation. The result? I fetched Dad beers, manned the T.V., and in exchange he let me mess up his hair while he watched the game.

We didn't play every weekend, but when the occasion arose, I couldn't be happier. With the fridge stocked, the T.V.

blaring, and Dad in an amiable mood, I was free to dive into my imaginary world without reservation.

And in that world, I was the proud owner of a sports bar that doubled as a barbershop. *Sally's Place*, as it was called (Sally was my business name), was the joint where every man in town came when he needed a haircut. *Sally's Place* looked like an old saloon, with dark wooden floors and a long bar against the back wall. There were no windows to cast a glare on the six big screen T.V.s, each broadcasting a different sporting event. At *Sally's* there was always lots of cheap, cold beer, and barrels of peanuts. And, of course, we encouraged tossing your empty peanut shells on the floor. Instead of tables or bar stools, the rest of the room was filled with large brown leather swivel chairs. *So*...you picked out the chair you wanted, swiveled it around to face the screen broadcasting your favorite sports team, I fetched your beer of choice, and then I began on the masterpiece that would become your hair. All of these amenities combined to give us an advantage over every other barbershop—or *bar* for that matter—in town.

In reality? Well, reality was never one of my favorite places, but for the purpose of accuracy, *Sally's Place* looked a lot more like our living room than a glorified sports bar. I used to put one of the wooden kitchen chairs in the middle of the room and face it toward the only (and small) T.V. we had. Then Dad would stroll in, like he'd pushed open old-fashioned saloon doors, and we'd exchange friendly greetings. He'd have a seat, and I'd drape a bath towel around his shoulders, clipping it behind his neck with my pretty pink hair clips. I'd hang my little purple spray bottle, filled with water, on the back of his chair, turn up the T.V., and grab him a can of our *one* variety of cheap beer from Mom's fridge. But every time I uttered those words, 'Can I get you a beer?' I felt tough and in charge.

Mom was not as big a fan of those 'beer fetching' words, but Dad thought it was cute. Besides, *Sally's Place* didn't have any other wait-staff or stylists, other than me, so Mom usually wasn't allowed prolonged stays in the living room while *Sally's* was open. It messed up my concentration, and it just wasn't part of the script.

So it was then. Armed with a brush, a spray bottle, Mom's hairspray, lots of baby barrettes, and a flare for the extraordinary, I was allowed on those perfect afternoons to turn Dad's thinning, straight hair into a ten-year-old girl's version of Hollywood pizzazz.

My most disheartening moment of the day always came when the fourth quarter time clock finally wound down to zero. Dad's game was over, and soon mine would be too. Just after the buzzer sounded, Dad would pretend to pay me. Then without fail he would walk immediately to my parent's bathroom to shower and wash out all my hard work. I hated that part, but I decided that this little insult was worth the three or four hours of fun I had before it came.

I learned to deal with rejection, and Dad learned to deal with spray bottles, tugging fingers, and little pink barrettes with poodles on them. This was our arrangement, and it suited us nicely.

I even gave Dad a perm one afternoon when he was being particularly oblivious to my busy fingers. That little experiment didn't go over quite as planned (Dad apparently didn't share in my excitement), and my masterpiece was washed out *before* the fourth quarter even started. After that, Dad made a few amendments to the 'rules' of our little charade, and after being closed for only a few weekends, *Sally's Plac*e reopened and play resumed.

Mom never quite understood how Dad survived all my tugging and experimenting on his hair, but it didn't seem to faze him. He was easy that way—*not* easy in all ways—but truly perfect when it came to pretend. For all of my growing up, Dad was unarguably my favorite playmate in all games of the imagination—and I had many, *many* games. Patterned after *Sally's* favorite customer himself, I was capable of turning all situations into new and uncharted worlds. Sometimes those worlds were more comforting than reality. Imagination can very powerfully hold a key to escape, and sometimes I let imagination hold me.

Real

We allow many things in the worlds of real and pretend to hold us. Things we give the power to grip our frames and keep us still or adversely to propel us forward. Sometimes such things are memories, feelings, places, people, joys, or grievances, but for me—and for my father—all have born one resemblance.

They have all been ruled by passion. Passionately is the way I was designed to live. This is a discovery I have only *very* recently made, but it is a reality that has been with me from my beginnings. It was the way of life I was born from, born into, and born *for*.

In my house we lived the all-or-nothing kind of way, and to this day, ambiguity, more than anything else, causes me to cringe. Although we had to build our lives among the ruins of many nothings, the nothings taught me that a dream that survives is worth it all.

I think that is why my father was so crazy about football. For those who played, dreams of victory never got lost in ambiguity. Every game produced one winner and one loser, and when confusion toward this end arose, the solution was an easy one: overtime. I knew Dad always wished his life could be like that. There were so many overtimes he never received, and unfortunately, he saw all those games as losses.

I clearly remember many of the game-days that Dad and I watched together. In a stadium seat or an old recliner beside my father, there were never dull moments. In fact, there were few moments of actual sitting. There was just too much excitement to warrant such passive participation. At an early age, decked out in obnoxious sports paraphernalia, I learned that nonpartisanship in football is not only boring but wrong. Real fans always choose a side. Where's the thrill if you are not screaming at the top of your lungs? When in doubt, my Dad taught me to always root for the underdog, and though he shared with me everything else he knew and believed about the game, this alone best defines the way my father lived.

Dad loved to see the misrepresented and the forgotten earn their way back into the memorable. I know that's how he thought of himself. He was an aged dreamer who desperately wanted to land somewhere back in his original paradise. He wanted to win that first, forgotten game. He didn't want to have to wish for overtime.

That first game had been played for Dad's heart; his life's dream. He had always wanted to become a sports announcer. Not just any announcer, mind you, but "the voice of the Green Bay Packers." That would have been all of heaven to him, but it was a heaven he never knew. No, Dad's dream fell prey to a very different voice: the voice of practicality and responsibility. Now that I am in my twenties, I finally understand just how crafty that voice can be. For Dad, the voice was played by a flag happy ref. He didn't seduce the dream, but instead, exhausted the will. Resistance is the difference between life and regret. My father always regretted the paradise he never fought for or believed in enough to venture out and find.

What did he find instead? I'm not sure that even he would have known how to answer that. But he tried. He tried to see traces of the dream in the life he led. I think that when he caught the shine of small glimpses, we caught it, too. It shone in him, and he could light up like no one else I've ever met. He could be the most excited and happy person—for no reason that my Mom or I could actually touch, though she and I tried to reach for it. We tried to grab hold of it, because we wanted all those smiles and that extraordinarily loud laughter to stay longer. Laughter is great medicine. We took it a lot, but we needed it a lot. Passion laughs like that. Passion takes its medicine in gulps.

My father introduced me to passion with every breath he took, but passion always has two sides. No one else can love like the passionate—it's magical, somehow—but nothing else can hurt so much as their words. It's a seesaw too heavily burdened to keep any balance. All that power can't help but cause the sway.

We all became gifted at the sway—I would have been seasick to stand still. Oh, there was never a lack of love. I always knew my Dad loved me—much more than he loved himself, if he even loved that man at all. Sometimes it was just hard to see his love for us: he hid it when he hid himself. Those were the moments when the seesaw tilted and we all fell to the bottom. The bottom is so cold, and when you're there, it can be hard to believe that the sway will ever bring you back up again.

But we still waited for the upward sway, and I hated the wait. I hated it so much that I began to compromise the highs. I didn't want to be up that high again, anymore. I just wanted the middle, the safety of life without sway, a life where highs never fall. Passion became the reality that scared me the most. I just wanted anything but the bottom; anything but the wait.

The bottom was coldest for my father. At the bottom even the smallest glimpses of his neverdream disappeared, and darkness replaced his shine. It was the darkness that hid him from us. He would steal his heart and leave us as the light faded out and his world became dead to him. He saw himself as a fallen star from a world that had once, long ago, been filled with light. Plainly, he saw himself as a failure, and most of all, a failure to everything worthy of love.

He felt unworthy. He fought love, because he had a sense that the right was not his. He could make it so hard for our love to reach him. With the years, my Mom and I found it harder and harder to make the push. Regardless, though, love is always the heart's desire.

I knew the chains and freedom of that desire well. With such an early and extensive introduction to the power and sway of passion, I knew that love without passion could never fill a heart completely—*but it wouldn't break it either*. I grew to despise anything that could not be controlled, and I tried, in vain to mold my own heart into a well-oiled machine of logical efficiency. Over time, my yearning for the kind of love that is deep with passion would continue to mount, but my fear of it would learn to compensate and hide impulses. With a great mistrust, I came to fear and desire passion more than anything else in life.

The fear was oppressive, and we were all so afraid. With its black cloak, fear hung over the heart of our home. My father was probably more afraid than any of us. He feared himself—and all his impulses—in an ever constant struggle. He knew love was the real underdog in our lives, and he desperately wanted it to get back on top. Still, even as he desired love to win, he couldn't stop punishing himself for the past. They were wounds he just wouldn't let heal. I grew under the care of a wounded player, and in so many ways, it is as simple as that.

His life taught me that only a fool believes that time is the healer of all wounds. It takes much more than time. Many of the wounds my father carried had known him longer than I had. Time was what Dad felt had run out on him. Time was what he was always trying to get back. So Dad lived his life in a place somewhere beyond time; a place where those without trophies go after the game and do not celebrate. He retired there—and my father never truly played again.

Love was the only inspirational Lombardi that could have pulled an aged man from a worn bench. However, the constant paradox of Dad's life kept him away from this long coveted victory. This is how he lived: only love could heal him, but it was only love that he wouldn't let try.

Top Hush

"I won't let you fall. I'm here to catch you. Just pretend like you're skating. Ready?"

"Yeah. OK, here I come."

Dad and I were standing in the middle of a huge snow field up about 11,000 feet in the middle of Montana's Beartooth Mountains. We were exploring, and I was about to ski down this mountain in my tennis shoes.

I had taken off, and what began as a delighted squeal suddenly changed into an urgent cry, reminding Dad of his promise. "I don't think I can stop … DAD!!!"

Thump! That was the solid sound as I collided with my father's legs and took him down. We slid a few more feet before we stopped, and then, grinning in a 'Mom-would-kill-us-if-she-saw-us' sort of way, we let ourselves inch forward to look over the edge of the snow cliff we had almost gone off.

Dad chuckled, "See, I told you I'd catch you."

"Yeah, I guess you did. Think those rocks down there would have hurt a lot?"

"Probably, but that's why I was here to stop you," and then, unnecessarily, he added one of our most frequently used disclaimers, "I wouldn't tell your mother about this."

"Right." Laughing and recovering the breath we had left caught up in our throats, we gave ourselves a minute to rest before we addressed the issue of how in the world we were going to get back onto dry ground. We never thought these things through ahead of time.

* * * * * * *

I remember that day like it was yesterday. There are very few moments in life that instantly become snapshots of pure happiness. That day is one of mine. I know that if I end up having one of those life-passing-before-my-eyes kinds of exits from this world, that day will be in the highlights. Actually the entire four weeks that my parents and I spent out west in the summer of 1989 were unforgettable.

My father loved no place on earth more than the West, and Montana especially. Mom and I loved it too; we couldn't help falling in love alongside him. When you saw the deep kind of refreshment that being there put in Dad's eyes, you *had* to join in.

We spent several summers out West, and I treasure those vacations like one treasures rare jewels. Under Western skies, our lives shone like diamonds, and it felt as if all the pressures of life had finally created something precious. Though I tried to control the urge, I couldn't help but wish we could stay forever. Every moment out West still glitters in my mind.

I think I was seven that particular summer, and it was

definitely a summer of many firsts for me. Just a few days before Dad's and my day of exploration, I caught my first fish. It was a small, but worthy rainbow trout that had given up its comfortable life in Rock Creek (the stream that ran by our cabin) so it could become a small trophy for me.

I remember being so excited about my fish and wanting Mom to see him that I forgot to sit him back in the water where he could breathe. At that age I didn't like the taste of fish, and I hadn't set out to keep any that I caught. Once it occurred to me that he had stopped flopping around and fighting our capture, I was very upset. By the time we reached Mom, I wasn't nearly as excited as I had been initially.

Mom, however, was quick with a suitable solution, as moms always are. She tried to persuade my troubled eyes, reasoning that no one lets their first fish go. Pictures of the first catch are a necessity, she insisted, and taking pictures keeps the fish out of the water for too long. She could see that I was not fully convinced, so she tried taking the blame herself in a final attempt to remove the murder charge to which I had already pled guilty. If only she had been there with the camera, she offered, we wouldn't have had to trek all the way to the cabin to show her my catch. This was *almost* enough to pacify my feelings of guilt—but not quite—so dad took the last step to recover my smile, and told me that he was really hungry for some rainbow trout. As matter-of-fact as it sounds, this met my approval, and I was finally persuaded that I had done something good. Later, the whole incident would become a bragging right for me. As for the evening at hand, choosing the next course of action was easy: in our all-or-nothing way, we celebrated.

We loved any excuse to celebrate, and later that night we extended our celebration by walking down to the laundry room in the basement of the hotel portion of the lodge. This may not sound like much fun, but I had discovered that the basement was full of surprises. I remember a pool table and a soft-drink machine that sold A&W cream soda. I've never again had cream soda that tasted so good and cold.

Consequently, we stopped needing the excuse of laundry to take this nighttime walk. Dad and I would take the long way, along the riverbed, and I always skipped on the return trip to the cabin. I have so many memories like this one from that summer, and all of them seem about perfect to me.

The crisp July day when Dad and I chose to begin our quest as Rocky Mountain explorers was no exception. That morning, the two of us got up early, packed a lunch, packed the rental car, and took off toward the top of the Beartooth Highway. This was *my* day, and I could choose any stopping point I liked to park the car and begin our hike. It was more than gorgeous that morning, and I could hardly keep my excitement from overpowering my small frame's feigned composure. Even the chipmunks perched along the stone wall we passed caused me to slip up and let out a little burst of giddy energy.

Dad was as silly and pumped as I was. There were really two kids going up the mountains that day, but in different ways. Dad wanted to feel young again, and I wanted to hurry and grow up. Days like that always made me want more days like that: going everywhere I had never been and seeing everything I had never seen.

The view from 11,000 feet is incomparable, and dreams are given limitless inflation there. From certain places in the Rockies you can see into more than one state and your heart can believe that the bounds of reality truly have fallen away.

Sometimes Dad and I stood silently beside one another, gazing out on the breathtaking view, and simply letting our hearts believe in dreams. The dreams he saw in those moments were dreams from his past, but when he looked at my dancing eyes, he saw the fresh face of possibility: things not yet seen. I bloomed so many seasons at once when we were up that high.

That day we shared a thousand stunning views and a thousand moments for dreaming. I still can't figure out how there was time to fit them all in. But then maybe that's why that day stands out so much to me. For a brief moment, time stood still, and we lived amongst the magical. Even the air felt supernatural as we walked upon it.

Dad thought so, too. In fact, the only times in my early childhood when I remember my father paying homage to, or showing a curiosity about, any kind of higher power was when we were atop a mountain somewhere out West. Maybe there were other times, but the first mention of His name that my heart actually heard and remembers was in the mountains. I can recall more than once Dad breaking into the perfect silence with these words, "I just feel like we must be closer to God up here." Then he'd ask me, "April, can you feel it?" And I could. I didn't really know what I felt, but I knew it was something beyond myself; something big and magnificent; something that if I saw it today, I would recognize as being full of His glory.

We bathed in His glory that day. It felt more like dancing than hiking, really. We didn't have much of an organized plan—spontaneity was the general rule in our family—but because of my recent fishing success, we *had* brought along our poles and lures. We soon discovered, however, that getting close enough for my tiny arms to cast the line into the un-weeded part of the glacier lake required waders—something we didn't have.

No problem. We easily abandoned our fishing aspirations for the broader ambitions of the true explorer. I liked carefree exploring better, anyway. Boldly, we headed off into the unknown. One by one, the challenges of building a bridge, mastering the art of tennis-shoe-skiing, and ascending the loftiest heights of the mountains arose before us.

Carrying big rocks from a quarry on one hillside and dumping them into the fast flowing stream we encountered, we accomplished our first task: the bridge. Our accomplishment soon enabled us to cross over to the snow fields my heart had already dove into. The whole building process was exhausting but thrilling, and when we reached the other side of the stream, we had a picnic.

After lunch, we at last started toward the snow. I

don't remember much about lunch, and I imagine I hurried it along. Finally we reached the top of the highest patch of white, climbing precariously from fallen boulder to fallen boulder. The incline was sharp, and we knew that down was the only way across. Oh, it could have been backwards, and I wouldn't have cared. It was snow; I was from Florida; this was my day with Dad; and if down was the only way across, then down was *exactly* how we would go—*no questions asked*!

I was quite insistent on our descent—and Dad loved it. He always did enjoy that fearless, and often stubborn, streak in me. When I wasn't being disobedient, my father encouraged my obstinacy. Contrarily, it has always scared my mother. Now that I am older, I think I recognize that my hard-headedness also caused my father to fear for me and my future. When I showed him that come-hell-or-high-water fire in my eyes, he knew that I would never be able to find satisfaction anywhere beyond the playing field. He knew I was hungry for the game. It was a hunger he had seen before...in himself.

He feared failure for me. Although he knew that I needed that fire for my life, the possibility that I could end up burnt-out and dark, like him, scared him to death. Still, he also knew that if I *did* ever make it to the trophy room, my life would be more beautiful and glorious than even the most perfect mountain top view. It would be the kind of life he once dreamed of for himself. So he prayed for my heart, he told me to dream, and he turned on himself for not being an example of dreams that had come true.

There was one big thing that Dad never realized about my dreaming. He overestimated me a little, or maybe he underestimated me. My first big dream was much simpler than he had imagined. It was him: I just wanted to make him happy as his daughter. Almost ten years later, when I finally told him that I had kept the memory of that day close to my heart as one of my favorite moments, he was shocked and speechless.

Dad never knew he could be a dream to anyone else. He had ceased being the starting player in any of his own dreams long ago. The best he imagined that he could do now was stand at the bottom of every snow field I decided to hurl myself off of, and be there to catch me if, or when, I started to fall. This was probably the hardest task he ever came up against. It is, in fact, a task too big for any mere man.

But a seven-year-old girl doesn't know that. When her Daddy caught her that day, he caught her heart, too. She placed her trust in him and believed in him. That was something he just never realized or wouldn't believe.

Loud Middle

For the most part, our lives didn't take place on mountain tops. The vacations of summer came only in their season, and the rest of the year we were forced to reside somewhere else. That somewhere had three bedrooms, two bathrooms, a family room, a living room, a dining room, a kitchen, and a back porch. Our house was normal in size, and we were a small family, but we occupied our space in a big way. Nothing was left vacant, whether it was a hallway closet or a lull in conversation, we knew how to fill it—and fill it to the max!

Dinnertime in my house was a good example of our space-filling capabilities. Most families sit down to the dinner table and enjoy give-and-take, civilized conversation. But not us. Although sitting down and eating dinner together as a family was always important in my house, the scene that played out when we finally did sit down more closely resembled a group of lawyers vying for a spot on the six o'clock news than a family meal. It was a contest to see who could be heard. Instead of probing for typical "how was your day?" responses, we answered voluntarily, competing over who could tell the biggest and best story. We filled our house with the roar of fanciful tales.

When my friends came for dinner, our story-telling had a comical effect on their un-expecting ears. They usually spent the whole meal in wide-eyed disbelief as they experienced the rapid volleying of conversation that overlapped and left them dizzy. For the rookie player, it was hard to keep up, and our three raised voices soon became to them one constant roar. Without meaning to, our unabashed eagerness produced a shy reserve in them. They became incapable of conversation—well, until they learned the rules of our dinner table games.

There was really only one rule—that *there were no rules*. For the friends that stuck around, their meek-and-mild phase of 'Jones' socialization earned them enough hours of observation to discover this secret. Soon, their voices added to the chaotic yelling. Some of my friends got so good at our game that we proudly adopted them into our dysfunction. Every all-star player became a beloved child to my mother. If you wanted to be heard in my house, you learned to be loud. It was simple, really—maybe not civilized—but simple.

My family has always been this way about everything. While some families struggle to communicate, we only struggled to communicate unselfishly. There was always contact being made; but sometimes it left a bruise instead of the caress love leaves. When it did caress—*it was really something*—but so was the pain. This is the way and sway of passion.

For our small family, even house cleaning produced violent waves. All of us hated the thought of cleaning.

Nonetheless, it couldn't be put-off forever, so Saturdays became the family workday in my house. I say "work" in the loosest sense, because there was always much more singing, dancing, and break-taking than cleaning. We seemed incapable of lifting a finger without the radio on. And when it was on, it was turned up so loud that each of us could hear it in our own remote jail cell of forced labor. That way, instructions barked across the house were never received—or their reception was, at least, deniable. We never *crossed* the house to engage in normal conversation. Our close-proximity yelling was practiced at dinner, so on Saturdays we worked on stretching our range.

Denying the reception of instructions wasn't the only good thing about loud music. The singing and dancing encouraged by the noise was even better. As we worked, each of us added our own voice and rhythm to the blaring music. Actually, I'd have to say that we sounded good for an unprofessional trio. I feel sure that the neighbors weren't left out of our Saturday morning ritual. Because of my family, the whole block grew up listening to the Beach Boys.

And really—that's all it took. If a classic like "Good Vibrations" came through our stereo speakers, we had a perfect reason to take a break. The break-taking, which was frequent, usually began with a great song and Mom being lost in one of the back-bedrooms. On these occasions, Dad and I met in the living room—in the center of the house and nearest to the stereo—and put on an impromptu interpretation of whatever song was playing. It was maddening fun, until we were *discovered*. We'd get the "*Te---d!*" and "*A---pr--il!!*" and then the "*What* are you two doing???" But Mom always knew good and well what we were doing. Our spontaneity was simply protesting the stick-to-it-ness that real cleaning requires. She knew so well, because one out of every three times, she joined in.

So it was in my house. We were all masterful at initiating breaks and accomplishing little. Even Mom had a bag of tricks. A tea break (as in hot tea) was her favorite scam, and Dad and I were always willing to comply. We are still avid tea drinkers in my house.

In the last few years, we expanded our horizons to include coffee along with tea. With the overnight popularity of espresso bars and a Starbucks on every corner, our break-taking tendencies never had it so good. Now, even on the road, we are presented with limitless time-wasting opportunities.

I continued to use the coffee reward system in college, and now in graduate school, to facilitate my studying. In wonderful carefree college, I controlled my short lapses of concentration with the promise that a grande latte would reward my diligence. But I usually gave in early. Then as I sipped my reward, I would get lost in my journal, creating a new song or poem. Before long, I had forgotten that I was supposed to be at a class, and honestly, most everything else was forgotten as well—everything except that my mug was empty and it had been a whole hour since my last shot of caffeine. It's a charming cycle; although, some of my friends prefer to call it a vice. *They*, however, did not go through Saturday morning training as I did. So as with those early beginnings, much fun is had and caffeine consumed, and very little is learned—at least in the way of school subjects. Unfortunately, in graduate school I have actually *needed* shots of caffeine for real studying. But it's really best not to talk about something so unpleasant.

Nonetheless, I trace my caffeine addition back to those frighteningly loud Saturdays when the Jones household transformed house cleaning into entertainment. The noise-level may have been unhealthful and nutrition lacking, but at least on those Saturdays our yelling was restricted to the topics of stereo volume and how much time had elapsed since our last break taken. Mom might have loosely played the role of taskmaster, but we were all in on the charade.

* * * * * * *

We were performers with a talent for noise. We had our chaotic conversations, but even when that wasn't center stage, the soundtrack played on. That's because my dad always had a game rocketing around on the TV screen. Even Dad's seat at the dinner table had a clear shot of every one of Joe Montana's Hail Marys to Jerry Rice. The 'Niners were my favorite when Montana quarterbacked.

If there wasn't a game on, there was still no need to fear the impending lull of a silent television. Chris Berman was usually available, via ESPN, to shout out something about a game already played or one soon to be played. I only ever wanted to watch highlights when he gave them.

Whether or not "he...could...go...all...the...way," got me every time.

So all the way that we went, we carried an announcer's voice with us. Much like cell phones today, in our house, the TV or radio always provided an extra voice and the possibility of escape or diversion. Each announcer sung out the play-by-play of our lives, and it felt like the ghost of Dad's dream was with us. The wins and losses came, and we stopped keeping score—but the competition was always full-throttle. Sometimes it was three against the world, and sometimes it was every man for himself. Still, there was very little time to pause; very little time to let the house get empty and quiet.

But it was so much more than a house. It was always a home; our home; my home. Yes, it was a fiery one, but fire warms at least as often as it burns. The one thing I *can* say with certainty about those early beginnings: Between my Mom, my Dad, and me, we never knew the meaning of dull or quiet.

* * * * * * *

I guess that's why, when I walked through the door one evening fifteen years ago, the single, eerie erupting sob I heard followed by complete, and thick, *silence* hit me harder than any loud noise we had ever made.

Silent Bottom

I stopped cold. I stood in the doorway, and suddenly it seemed that our hallway led to nowhere. Something in me had felt the wrong when I first stepped over the doorframe, and now I didn't want to know; I didn't want to encounter whatever lay just a few steps down the hall.

Then I saw him. My father was walking towards me. His eyes were red and his face flushed. It took a minute to register the obvious: Dad had been crying. Only one other time in my eleven years had I witnessed a tearful sheen to my father's eyes, and then we had been gathered with family to bury Dad's mother.

But here he was. Standing like me now: stuck in a hallway that was quickly closing in. Mom had not followed him, but I knew she was in their bedroom where they had most likely been crying together. It was *her* sob that I had first heard and *her* sob that triggered the silence that now hung between Dad and me. I noticed that the shine was gone from Dad's face. He looked tired—and suddenly old.

I was scared.

But the silence was fading. What was there to say, except that which couldn't be left unsaid? So my father took a heavy breath and let his words make, swiftly, their incision on both our hearts. "April," he began, "I have cancer."

Like that—the world changed.

But as the words fell, I did not gather them to me to wash with tears. I said nothing. My eyes glazed over and I somehow willed my body to obey; ordered my legs to move. Giving my father a look that couldn't have seemed brave, I brushed past him into the dining room. There I remained, begging not to be touched or embraced, lest my strength fail.

I remember only two thoughts circulating through my head. One it would take me years to forgive myself for, and the other built the first layer of the wall I would allow to be put up around my heart.

I heard "cancer," but I thought, "death." What kind of cancer was this? Would it kill him? ...Was it something he would pass on to me?? I couldn't stop that last thought from taking shape in my mind, but I regretted it as soon as it arrived. How could I think such a thing when my father was so sick? How could I be so selfish? I didn't dare voice my thoughts, but then they were answered, anyway. I hoped desperately that Dad had not read my mind, and I cursed myself for feeling so relieved.

As dread and relief came and went, another thought, a resolution, was already claiming lordship over my emotions. I had heard my mother's uncontrollable sob; I had seen my father's red eyes and heard the quiver in his voice: I had seen strength fail. *Strength could not fail*. Someone had to be strong. Someone had to hold the fragile together. Stepping forward, and leaving my father alone in the hall, I vowed it would be me. I did not shed a single tear that night. I swallowed every lump in my throat, and I made myself busy, very busy.

I had an English project due the next day. Like blinders on a horse, I saw only the work I had to do in front of me, and I welcomed, totally, its consumption of my thoughts.

... the Wait

I was riding to school with Courtney that morning. I walked through the doorway without knocking. No one ever knocked at the Johnson house. Vanna, their dog, was there at the door, and she greeted me with goofy merriment. Maybe I patted her head. I don't know. Her wagging tail struck me as out of place.

I headed straight for the back of the house where I knew Courtney would be hastily getting ready in her bedroom. She'd be running late, re-trying on a shirt she had already tried on four times, and finishing last-minute grooming details that just never even occurred to me until I saw her perform them. As I made my way to her bedroom I looked down, for the first time, at what I was wearing. I didn't remember getting dressed that morning, but apparently I had: jean shorts and a regular shirt; nothing special. That was good. I felt too strange to want to be noticed.

I paused outside her door, but I knew she had already heard me coming down the hall. So without a chance to prepare any kind of speech, I made myself step inside. I gave her only half a second of eye contact, but it was all I could handle; and then plopped down on her bed. In that short moment, nothing brilliant filled my vacant mind, so I shrugged at the questions her eyes were darting in my direction, and simply handed her the note my dad had written for me to give my teachers. It read:

To Whom it May Concern:

Last night I returned from my doctor's visit with Dr. Cowin. Dr. Cowin had removed a mass from my right shoulder on Fri. Feb. 18th. Yesterday the lab report came back from Shands and it was not good. The diagnosis was a Malignant Lymphoma. We were all upset so any work April did not complete was directly a result of this news. Please be understanding with her for the next couple of days.

At this point the outlook is good and this type of cancer is treatable and sometimes curable. We feel things will work out fine, but it will be hard on her at first.

Thanks,

Ted Jones

Courtney's hand went to her face. "Oh April!" Then she paused, and we stared at each other, motionless. "I'm so sorry," was all she could get out. She hugged me. I tried to stiffen up, but I couldn't stop my shoulders from shaking twice. She could see that I didn't want to talk about it, and I didn't want to cry before school, so she brushed the hair from my face and went to her dresser for supplies. She silently packed her older sister's concealer in my backpack for the unspoken possibility of future tears. Then we walked out of the house together—or she walked out of the house, and I was brought with her.

Courtney took care of me that day. She handed Dad's letter to each of our teachers and stood as bodyguard, intercepting any words of sympathy that threatened to bring an onslaught of emotional instability. I didn't know at the time what the letter said, but Courtney told me it explained everything well, and I believed her. I didn't want to read it; I didn't want to encounter the facts again. I just wanted to wake up from this day. Mostly, I wanted it all to go away.

* * * * * * *

Nothing went away, but maybe it got easier. It's hard to say. Or maybe we became numb. Still, you can't be completely numb to the lurking presence of an unwanted guest such as death himself. Death is *never* welcome, and *never* can we be fully desensitized to his intent. He has one intent and one intent, alone: to devastate.

How I hated death. People say that hate is too strong a word, but it's not too strong when it's exactly how you feel. Death would not leave us, and the hate would not leave my heart. It grew until I could not bear its burden. I wanted to fight death. I wanted to send it to hell. I wanted to gain love and hope and everything that could spit in its face—but I did not know where to find them or how to keep them close once I had them within my grasp. I needed, desperately, to grip life and to hold on with all the life I had left.

MORE

Power

For two and a half years after college, I lived on the North Shore near Boston. Storms there are of a whiter, colder nature, than they were growing up in Florida. As a result, I became adept with a shovel, window scraper, and pushing the tiny buttons on my cell phone with oversized, gloved fingers. For this Florida girl, these are big accomplishments. Truly, every day that I resisted shaking an angry fist at an overcast sky I considered myself 'jolly' and taking it well.

One such winter afternoon, the cold, brisk wind of an approaching storm seemed to bring with it memories and reflections. As I so often do, I sat down at my laptop and let my winter feelings find their way onto the page...

I'm working now on my second winter in the Northeast, and the "You'll get used to it" condolences are still coming. Oh, the unrelenting persistence of these New Englanders is sometimes more than I can take. "Maybe I don't want to get used to it!" I want to tell them. "Being warm, wearing tank tops and flip flops, and seeing sunshine—these are not ridiculous desires.

Most people prefer shorelines without ice on them, you know?! Beaches made for bare feet…those are real beaches! And by the way, you can keep your quaint, little fishing towns, because we both know you're just going to move to Florida when you retire anyway!" These are the things I sometimes wish I could scream at my fellow man suffering here on the lovely North Shore.

Of course, I never do—I can't. Why? Because I am a Southerner, and we Southerners prefer a little beating-around-the-bush, good-tempered technique my mother liked to call tact. It's just not in me to give it to them in the true Northern way; it goes too much against the grain. So instead I smile, and offer the answer to a question I am asked much too often, "No, I am not from here."

The weather, however, is not the only thing here that's cold. I loathe the rude blaring of car horns filling endlessly busy streets. I am offended by the inconsiderate shoving of unremorseful briefcases and shoulders that jolt you on sidewalks and never turn around to see if you're all right. Yes, all these things annoy me greatly. However, more than anything in New England—I absolutely, without a doubt, hate doors. They hurt my feelings. They make me feel invisible. Sometimes, when one more door—of a countless number of un-opened, or dropped, doors—stares, or slams, me in the face, I feel like I hear the voice of my grandfather, Honey, coming to my aid all the way from beneath the Georgia clay. With the crisp, gently powerful voice of a Southern gentleman, he firmly and with indignation takes up my cause, even if only within my memory, "DAMN YANKEES!" Such crass words, but they comfort me nonetheless. I feel that my honor has finally been defended, and I am a lady again. Someone has opened a door for me, even if he is only within my heart.

So as you might imagine, in this busy, cold, New England world, I am not exactly thrilled when I hear someone saying (on the other side of a door), "I think a storm is coming in," or "Looks like snow," or my favorite, "Better stock up on water, I hear a Nor'easter is coming our way, and you'll probably get snowed in—might even lose power." They really ought to say, 'you'll probably get snowed in—might even lose composure, or sanity, or any number of valuable, dignified things.' Oh how I hate the North!

* * * * * * *

But believe it or not, there was a time, long ago, when I actually thrilled at the words, "Looks like a storm." When I was growing up in Florida, discounting hurricanes, storms were one of my favorite happenings. Florida has fantastic thunder storms—and so many of them. We used to say during the summer that you could tell the time by the look of the sky. It always seemed to rain at 4 o'clock, on the dot, and I loved that dot! The crack of the thunder and the magnificence of the lightning—there was nothing I liked more than sitting on the front porch with my dad watching black clouds roll in and anticipating the frenzy that soon would be unleashed above our house.

This is an odd concept to most, because many people are scared of thunder and lightning. I, however, am fascinated, and since Florida is the lightning capital of the world, I have had countless opportunities to explore my fascination.

Maybe it comes from my father. Maybe this, too, is an area where our all-or-nothing way has had sway on my life. I've never wanted to witness a gentle rain. I don't care for showers that simply water the ground—slowly, drizzling—until scattered, grayish clouds finally dissipate. No! I want roaring thunder, powerful winds, flashing lightning, and wild, unharnessed havoc. *That's* a storm. That's incredible. That's perfect.

My Mom never understood this obsession—or maybe she did, yet it just frightened her too much. She'd come to the front door, "Ted! Come on, now. Won't you come inside? And April—do you really think it's a good idea for you to have her out here?"

"But Mom—"

Ignoring me, "Ted, did you hear that thunder? Look at that lightening! I think it's close. Shouldn't you be coming inside soon?"

Reluctantly, Dad would finally give in, and we would ease Mom's anxieties by bringing the lawn chairs back inside. Yet even then, I would take up my post near the biggest window, eyes glued to the sky, silently praying for the electricity to go out. I don't wish for this on the North Shore, because unlike warm Florida, when the power goes out in New England, you freeze to death!

But how I used to love when the lights flickered off—*then on—then off*—and the whole house became dark. Whenever this happened, Mom would bring out the old oil lamps, we'd feast on peanut butter or potato chips for dinner, and no one would have anything they needed to be doing or anywhere they had to be, except for simply sitting together—laughing and talking. Sometimes we'd play a board game, sometimes the lights would come on too soon and interrupt a perfect interlude, but whatever happened, it was always exciting, if just for a moment.

Watching the storms roll in with Dad was one of the highlights of my growing up years. The glory we watched together was unmistakable. I'd wish that experience on anyone—even all these Yankees.

Believing

While I loved a perfectly black sky, some of our sunnier traditions also hold a special place in my heart. One that stands out most in my mind is college game-day with Dad—specifically, going to the University of Florida to watch the Gators play. Spending a game-day with my father was always an unforgettable experience, and driving up to Gainesville for a Gator game exemplified this truth most.

My mother says that I once had a shirt that read "Semi-gator" across the front. This meant that I was the offspring of a Seminole alum and a Gator alum. As for this kind of open confession, it was one that was soon to pass. By the time I was five, Dad had already indoctrinated me with the code of the orange and blue, and I knew every Gator cheer by heart. I was appropriately repulsed by the combination of the colors garnet and gold (FSU), red and black (UGA), and orange and white (UT—Vols that is). I wanted nothing more than to be a University of Florida graduate, and so my mother's hopes were dashed: I was to be a Gator, and there was no turning back.

As for Saturday home games, I laugh now remembering all the superstitions my imaginative, young self built up. Let me explain by taking you through a typical Gator Saturday, when a well executed game-day would have gone something like this...

First my father insisted that we leave the house on time, and by on time, I mean ridiculously early. Game-day was probably the only time that my father and I agreed on the need to be punctual. If we did not leave on time, *by his clock*, then we would never have enough time, *by my clock*, to fit in all my superstitious activities.

So if kickoff was at 3:30, we were in the car by 9, and two hours later (taking all back roads and hitting game-day traffic only at the last possible minute) we would pull into the parking lot of Sonny's Real Pit Bar-B-Q for a greasy, satisfying bite to eat. It was imperative, according to my agenda, that Hazel be our waitress and that we sit in a booth. I even had specific booths that I preferred, but it all depended on the size of the Sonny's crowd.

When Hazel *was* our waitress, she was always excited to see us. Each September, when we drove up for our first game, we would walk into Sonny's, look around for Hazel, and then we'd hear her crossing the room calling out, "Oh my goodness! My how she has grown! It seems just like yesterday that she was barely big enough to sit in these booths! Well it's just sooo good to see y'all." Hazel was that grandmothering type: sweet and friendly, and always able to make you feel right at home. Dad said that Hazel had been waitressing since he was in college in Gainesville. I don't know if that was true, but it seemed like it could have been.

It was Hazel's way to refer to Dad as "Hun," or, "Hunny," and she always call me "Darlin'." I liked the sound of familiarity in those names, much like I valued the consistency of ordering the same meal time after time. From year to year, as if we sat in her section a couple days a week instead of just five or six times a season, Hazel would remember my order, calling it out as she wrote down, "One quarter chicken, white meat, double the fries, hold the slaw, and you'll need a big glass of sweet tea. I'll have it right out for ya, Darlin'." It was always a bad sign if Hazel wasn't working on a Saturday. With the Gators' game-day victory and our pleasurable lunch experience at stake, I took her absence to heart.

Sonny's was only our first stop of the day. After our meal, my superstitions got worse. While Dad paid at the counter, the next, and possibly most important, superstition was indulged. With Bar-B-Q chicken in my belly, next came the perfected practice of partaking of York peppermint patties! It was standard protocol that after a hearty lunch at Sonny's Dad would purchase exactly three York peppermint patties and hand them to me. Then carefully, and strategically, I unwrapped them one by one: eating them slowly and meticulously so that they lasted right up until we arrived at the stadium. If I timed it just right, the Gators were guaranteed a win. If not—everything was up in the air.

For the assurance of a win, there could be

absolutely no cheating, which, mind you, was not easy for me. My timing had to be perfect: no pause in eating, no saving the last bite in my pocket, no short cuts, no allowances. It only worked if my execution was perfect. I was hard on myself this way.

But sometimes honest efforts, or dishonest ones for that matter, simply became impractical. I couldn't control everything. If it was too hot outside, the third patty might melt in my hand or my pocket. Or, if we were too early for the game and found parking easily, then we'd have to make unscheduled stops on-foot to use up extra pre-game moments. Sometimes, even when we were right on time, it was impossible to make my peppermints last until we walked under the concrete "Gate 2." So of course, that is why it was so important to make the effort in the first place; and also why we were guaranteed a win if I were to succeed.

When Dad and I did have time to kill, we usually spent it at the Student Union. On the ground floor there was, and still is, a game room equipped with pool tables and bowling alleys. We didn't take up pool for some time (I was too small to reach over the table), but I spent many Saturdays with Dad bowling my little heart out.

Dad was exceptionally good at bowling, just as he was good at pool. It seemed to me he was good at most things. I, on the other hand, had not been blessed with these 'game' talents, but oh how I tried! Each new Saturday of the season, each fresh score sheet, I hoped and believed that my luck was about to change. I'd try on three pairs of bowling shoes before picking just the right pair, and then I'd spend the next ten minutes going up and down the shelves at the back of the lanes, trying to pick out the perfect, but manageable, bowling ball.

I was always drawn to things that were pink or some other girly color, but when it came to bowling balls I tried desperately to resist these urges. I wanted to be good—*tough* and *serious*—so I tried to settle on a green or red ball. Unfortunately, my hands were so small and my arms so tiny that I found myself with very few choices, as to color or otherwise. They just didn't make bowling balls my size. But I didn't want a kiddy ball. I wanted a grown-up's bowling ball. Dad said you needed weight to knock down the pins, and I was just not very good at knocking down those pins. I needed all the help I could get, and I was sure I needed a bigger bowling ball if I were ever going to prove myself at Gator Alley. So, stubborn to the core and unpersuaded by Dad to find a size suitable for me, I usually ended up with a ball much too big.

To add serious insult to injury, Dad and I had discovered long-ago that the lanes in the Student Union were not perfectly level. About three quarters of the way down, there was a slight bow in the old wood—a problem that I believe has since been fixed. For bowlers as good as my father, this was of no consequence. With enough speed on the ball, such a slight deviation doesn't impair your game. However, when you are roughly 40 pounds and can barely lift your bowling ball, an obstacle such as this is a much bigger issue.

So every time I thought I was going to get a pin, *maybe even more than one*, the three-quarter mark factored in. I did everything Dad told me to do—started back from the line, approached with confidence, drew back the ball, and released so that my ball went right between the arrows he recommended—but always, *always*, my efforts were to no avail. Time after time my hopes were dashed, as my wrong-size, ugly ball hit that warped wood and fell solidly into the gutter. With the sound the ball made as it fell and the absence of that cracking sound that a ball *ought* to make against white pins, I plodded, defeated, back to the bench. Bowling at Gator Alley could be quite damaging to my confidence.

Whether we bowled or not, there was only one more tradition to honor as a necessary part of our pre-game adventure. At some point, between the car and the stadium, we *had* to stop at the Hub (now the University Bookstore since its remodeling and relocation). At the Hub, only one item was on our shopping list: a button for my shirt and my collection. Every game I got a new button. They were inexpensive, most were silly, but each was vital to the Gators' success—and I wore them all! Before every game, Mom helped me fasten ALL my buttons to the front of my shirt. The sheer quantity of buttons weighed down my T-shirt so much that Mom bought me a pre-brassiere undershirt to wear underneath it. I not only had a lot of buttons, I had a lot of different types of buttons. One button sang out our fight song when you pressed the back, and another lit up with flashing lights. I used the latter feature for night games only, and sparingly, because I was so afraid the battery would run out. My most obscene buttons were in reference to the 'Noles or sometimes the Bulldogs, but my favorite cheer remains to this day, "It's Great to HATE, Florida State!" Oh my poor mother—stuck helping me fasten buttons that insulted her kind, but she was always a good sport.

My buttons were so obnoxious and in such supply, that I became known to some in our stadium section as the button girl, and would often be greeted as such on our way to and from the stadium. I think back now—if they had only known about the peppermints! I shouldered a lot of responsibility with my game-day superstitions.

And this is kind of the mentality I have always had. "*I can do it*; I can make it happen. I *have* to do it; I have to make it happen. Things and people and happiness are *depending on me*!" But my shoulders always were, and still are, much too small.

L i m i t s

It is funny that a person who began high school weighing less than 100 lbs. and standing only five feet tall, on a good day, *with shoes*, could believe that she could shoulder the world. But I did.

I did, and I worked very, very hard at it.

In seventh grade, I started going to the high school gym with my Dad in the evenings to lift weights. When he was coaching football, his offices were in the locker/weight room, so we spent a lot of time there. Even today, the musty smell of sweat and dirty football pads is comforting to me. Don't get me wrong—I don't want to wear it as perfume—but there's something that is comforting, nonetheless.

It may seem strange that as young as seventh grade I was working out. But you didn't know my dad. I was still going through puberty, and was skinny as a rail, but even a scrap of a woman can lift weights.

Besides, Dad and I always thought we were bigger than we actually were. At five feet, five inches, Dad was very stocky and built, but he still wasn't big. And me? Well, I was his petite, adolescent daughter—smaller than he had been at my age, and not destined to show him up as a grown woman. We were small. By all the world's standards we were less than average and maybe even insignificant, but that's a concept I've never been able to comprehend. Heart can make up for a lot of what a person might lack in size, and in the area of heart (imagination, passion, and all the like) Dad and I could always hold our own.

So for us, lifting weights really wasn't a strange father/daughter activity at all. Lifting weights represented discipline to my father. The weight room was a realm where he was in control and where he gained strength, and this powerful sense of refining the self was something my dad wanted me to experience. Neither of us was concerned about my losing weight or getting toned: I was a skinny, miniature 12-year-old for cryin' out loud, but learning the value of sweat and hard work was something to be gained.

In fact, exercise has taught me a lot about myself and is something I think I will always enjoy. As my father's daughter, my biggest struggle has been not motivation, but knowing my limits. I have several friends who frequent the weight room and excel in this area. But not me. I think, why go if I'm not going to push myself? Only 10 minutes left on the treadmill doesn't mean "I've already done 20, I can ease up now and start to cool-down." No! It means "crank up the resistance and crank out another mile or another 100 calories—*at least*!" If I can give only 20 minutes, I'd rather not go at all. This all-or-nothing thinking has been my biggest exercise downfall.

This kind of thinking (and the fact that I actually hate treadmills and prefer to run outside) is why sticking to any kind of exercise routine as an adult has been difficult. In Boston I was a full-time graduate student, I worked 10 hours a week for the family I lived with, I was in a serious dating relationship, and it was *freakin'* cold outside. The point: *I had no time*, and I *hate* being cold! Where I live now in Texas, I am a full-time law student, I work when I can, and I am married to the love I found in Boston. The point: *I have even less time*, and *I'm out of practice*. But I really miss those long runs, battling myself when trying to increase reps and weights, and having sore, tired muscles that put me to sleep. The knots in my shoulders, the hours I sit typing and reading, the amounts of coffee I drink and my restless sleep, are all clear indicators that I need to resume an exercise routine. And so I am learning that in this area a little bit of something would be better than a whole lot of nothing.

TIME

Resisting

(...the almost present)

Today, 11:00 a.m. is early, and my college roommate's Chihuahua, Casey, is an unwelcome "good morning." After 30 minutes of hopeless resistance to the inevitable, tossing in sheets the sun has intrusively warmed and hiding from a barking, wiggling dog who has decided to spit bathe me before I bathe myself, I begin to realize that I'm getting in on the day late. The sun seems to be saying, "The day started a while ago, kiddo, and you weren't up."

So I surrender, and I let the shower do the final convincing. I hate losing, but hot water has a way of reminding me that I made objectives for this day, and it's time to get a move on. And soon enough, that 'move on' has me in the motion of routine.

What shall I wear? I hate this question, but I regrettably waste a lot of my waking hours occupied with its solution. It's hard to remember when I just rolled out of bed and went. But today I answer the question more easily than usual. Draped over the chair are the jeans I only wore for three hours yesterday; those will do. And then the discovery that I only have one clean bra, my red one, seals the deal: red shirt, jeans, sweater, and comfortable shoes as a gesture to my tender feet. Time for make-up, no time for hair, so it goes up, and I'm out the door.

Hand on the doorknob, backpack on my shoulder, I hear, "April, you are always so put together."

That's a shock, but I pause and smile at my roommate's guest, Megan. "Thanks," I offer, "I guess it's just habit." I linger for a polite and sociable pause, offering the goodbyes and have-a-good-days, but then the door is shutting behind me, and I'm in my car.

I'm thinking about Megan's words as I drive. Put together? Always? Today was a disheveled and thoughtless morning in my personal view. But it didn't show. I guess it seldom does. Habit, I told her. I know that's true, and then I have one of my alien moments when I remember how much these friends don't know about my life—things I've never *really* told them. They don't know the *why* of most of me, but then I kind of like the weightlessness of that reality. Maybe I breathe easier in it.

And as I exhale deeply, I pull in the parking lot of Starbucks. Some things don't change. I'm still intimate with caffeine. Now, what were today's moderately motivating objectives I outlined in the shower? Oh right, to study, study some more, and study again. But I hate to study. Frankly, I'm just not that good at it. I get distracted. I come here for the taste of my doppio espresso more than its effect on alertness. Still, I need to accomplish a lot today. More than a lot, and yet...*just ten minutes later*...here I am, letting my thoughts find their way onto my computer.

It's refreshing to be here writing again. It's been a while since I gave this my full attention, and today could be the worst and best timing: worst, because my assignments won't wait for my typing fingers to dawdle, but also best, because I've missed the opportunity to be me. I am most completely me when I sit typing, just like this. That's when I *feel* the most put together. For me, words are honest.

I know in about a minute guilt will get the better of me and I'll return to being April Jones, college senior, scholarly and 'serious' student, taking her last 15 hours at the University of Florida. But that's not this minute. This minute I'm letting the only real passion in my life take over. I'm writing, and so I guess I'm being me for a change.

* * * * * * *

Now back to my story? I can't help the temptation to skip this part. We've covered the beginning, so why not skip to some of the more recent years like I just did? The almost present of college, or my time thereafter in Boston, or the recent move to Texas—*these could be interesting, too, right*? But I know the middle matters too much. I know that in the middle, beginnings and ends get all jumbled and confused. Up is down, down is up, and it's all relative, but I really wouldn't be at the end without the middle. So I'll do it. I'll go there again, and I'll tell you. No, I'll take you back with me. I'll try to remember and not hurt so much while I write.

But I know that's not very likely.

Growing

Monday nights.

I'll start with Monday nights...

...and my parents and I are at Tony's Pizza and Subs. We seat ourselves in a booth near the back (which isn't all that far from the front), and Rhonda comes over to take our order. No menus are passed out—we are regulars—and she has brought our three unsweetened teas. There are two lemons on Mom's tea, none on mine, and Mom is passing out sweet 'n' low. It's a normal Monday.

We love Tony's. It's a typical, small-town Italian joint, but it's our place. The booths are red, postcard views of the Mediterranean are painted on the walls, there's always just one or two waitresses, *max*, you pay at the counter, everyone's a local, and all the food is made with the two g's: garlic and grease. It's modestly located to the side of the corner Jiffy (well, it was always the Jiffy, but now I think it's a Lil' Champ), and while that might deter some people, in Eustis we know that the best food doesn't come in a frilly package. Besides, Tony's location provides one-stop-shopping for a lot of the regulars: dinner for your gut, gas for your truck, and you can even pick up a gallon of milk to replace the carton you ran out of this morning. That's if you drink milk, which we don't.

In fact, we don't cook either. Mom gave it up a while back. She says it was for Lent, but she is about as Catholic as the Dalai Lama. The truth is, after a long day at work, making it longer by working in the kitchen is the last thing she wants to do. "Why cook when you can eat out?" she says. And on Mondays, Tony's is our eatery of choice.

On this particular Monday, I am intently examining our table's parmesan cheese. The shakers here are always clogged, but I am learning how to conquer them. When those delicious garlic rolls—hot, glistening, dripping, pungent rolls—finally arrive at the table, I will be ready for them. In anticipation, I recreate the Tower of Pisa with parmesan cheese on a napkin. Then I tear down my tower as I coat every inch of my roll in parmesan. *Then I rebuild*, for roll number two.

I order and eat my baked spaghetti, "Rhonda, can I have fewer noodles and extra sauce, please?" I have a few more garlic rolls, and then I finish my second iced tea. When we're done, we'll hop in the car, drive not even a mile down the road, and my parents will drop me off at a small church for the middle school youth group.

This is the pattern for our Mondays, and I'm almost not sure how we settled into it. Eating at Tony's isn't too much of a stretch—we don't eat here only on Mondays—but the whole church thing kind of snuck up on us. Courtney was the first to invite me. Like my family,

Courtney's doesn't attend this church; however, her older brother goes for youth group, or Club as it's called. He started going with his best friend (whose family does attend) when he was in sixth grade. He loves it, and the summer before sixth grade, Courtney and I knew we had to get in on the fun. Why? Two obvious reasons: to be cool and meet boys. Boys are our main topic of discussion and the main source of our desire and confusion. They are disgusting; they are cute; they are weird; and we want to get their attention—although I cannot really say why.

So we go to church. It's kind of ironic, I guess. Or maybe not. Looking back I think, "At that age, are there any better motivators than boys?" What am I saying? Those are always the best motivators. In my twenties, boys were still weird, and I still wanted to be around them—most of the time.

So whether my intentions were honorable or not, church wove its way into my life, and the Monday routine into our family's pattern. The way Monday looked, and the way I looked on Monday, is what changed over the years. My growing up and growing pains can be captured in still frames of dinners at Tony's.

Early middle school Mondays consisted of parmesan cheese, garlic rolls, baked spaghetti, and a lack of attention to my personal appearance. By eighth grade, I had begun to dab some of the grease off the rolls with napkins. By ninth grade, parmesan cheese was over, and a well dabbed and scrutinized roll *might* be consumed if I was in a careless mood. Regardless, a ten-minute pause to primp in the Tony's bathroom could be counted on. During that ten minutes, I would actually use their public restroom to brush my teeth and gargle. It was a family tradition that my parents embarrassed me any, and *every*, chance they got, but when I started coming to Tony's armed with my toothbrush, toothpaste and a very large bottle of Listerine, it was their turn to wear the looks of chagrin. Another interesting change was evolving in that first year of high school: I got to know boys who drove cars. Now the teeth brushing and gargling took on new meaning which was not missed by my parents.

"Can Barry take me to Club?"

"No."

"Well, can he take me home?"

"I don't think so."

"Pleeeeaaaasssse!" trying to conceal the gargantuan bottle of Listerine that was next to me on the booth, and also the incriminating, untouched, bad-breath rolls that glared at me from the table.

My parents exchanged uncomfortable looks.

"Dad, it's just Barry. He *is* my boyfriend, and you like him."

"Well, I guess he can take you home, but we're dropping you off. And I want you in the house by 9:30. If he wants to see you more, he can come inside, and y'all can visit in the living room."

Uhhhhh. I hate sitting with my boyfriend and parents in the same living room. Then I can't sit close to Barry. Nobody else's parents act like this, and I hate telling Barry I have such an early curfew; it makes me feel stupid and immature. "Ok, fine. So can we go already?" If I have to be home early, I might as well get there to hang out before Club starts."

"Not until I pay the bill."

So it went...Mondays lost much of that early simplicity, and they never really went back to simple. There were other things that didn't go back, either. Like my hips, my thighs, my butt, my breasts, those definitely forsook the going back. And my sixth grade metabolism—I really miss that.

Barry? He took on a new name. There were more names than one, and the older I got, the more I appreciated those early curfews my parents had so stringently enforced. There may have been a lot of names in my early years, but there wasn't a lot of pain; there weren't the mistakes that could have been. I remember a journal entry from the beginning of my sophomore year of college that read, "His name was Barry; his name was Richard; his name was Craig; his name was Cody. A silly girl just gets older." That's probably accurate.

But putting those names aside, the two male figures that actually made the biggest impact as I was growing up weren't boyfriends or crushes. These two didn't care if my teeth were brushed, my hair fixed, or my makeup on. They didn't know love required any of these things. One of them didn't really understand love at all. The other loved so wholly, He required nothing of me, but gave all of Himself.

Turning

I am *almost* 13.

At this age, I was never just 12. Never 14, or simply 15. I was *almost* 16; I was 14 *and a half*; I was 15 *in a month*! And so, for this special moment, this pivotal chapter in my life, I am *almost* 13. Almost 13...and very afraid, very lonely, and full of questions.

And so I carried my fearful questions all the way to Mexico. A sheltered, American, almost-13-year-old decided to leave her parents at home and go to Mexico. Practically speaking there is no satisfactory answer to why. But sometimes practical is overrated—or you could say that it is *im*practical to try to be practical. And so, on a mission trip to serve the poor and share the gospel—a poor I had never seen nor desired to serve, a gospel I did not believe in or understand, with a church where I wasn't a member and didn't even attend regularly—I arrived in Rio Bravo, Mexico, without a clue why I had come.

The month before my arrival in Rio Bravo was a hectic one. A girl who had never hammered a nail—*tried*. My parents gave desperate looks, wrung their hands, and struggled to remember why they had said I could go on this trip. I sent out last minute letters to raise money for the trip, and all our family and friends wondered when April Jones, almost 13, had developed such humanitarian spirit. About this, I also wondered.

It was all strange. Why did I feel so strongly that I had to go on this trip? The group would depart for Mexico on the day of my thirteenth birthday. I was almost 13! I was almost a TEENAGER, and I was willing to miss it! By begging to leave with them, I was asking to enter my teenage era unheralded, without most of my friends, on an airplane, and certainly without cake. I think I found the lack of cake the most distressing.

I had always been stubborn when I felt strongly about something, but why did I feel so strongly about Mexico? Whatever the reason, something about this trip made my jaw lock, my back straighten, and my fists clench. Come hell or high water, I was going to Mexico. Of *that* I was certain—even if I didn't know why.

But soon, with or without a reason, everything to get me ready for the trip fell into place. First, all my money came in. In fact, I received twice as much support as I needed, so the surplus went to funding some of the other kids' trips. Second, my parents appeared to have semi-adjusted to the idea of my being in a foreign country, and Mom was mentioning guerrilla warfare and my being in danger only about once a week now. It looked like everything was in order!

Everything, except one thing, of course…that age-old question, *what was I going to wear*?!? But before my self-conscious, pubescent self could give it another thought, Mom was on it! My Mom had suddenly been inspired by domesticity and had undertaken the task of making my work clothes for the trip. Although I lived in central Florida (a place with a latitude very similar to Rio Bravo's), my mother, who had never been to Mexico, insisted I was unprepared for how insanely hot it was going to be. To complicate things, the church was requiring guys and girls, alike, to wear long pants on the work site for the sake of modesty in a foreign culture. Under these conditions then, my mother insisted, if I had any hope of avoiding heat stroke, I needed clothes of sensible, breathable, cotton...the perfect fabric that only a very lucky shopper could hope to find.

Lucky for us all, my mother was just that—a *very* lucky and talented shopper. So armed with all her tricks of the trade, she went out and bought fabric: cheap, cotton, sensible fabric. She found enough of this cheap, cotton, sensible fabric to make each day's work outfit from different material. Tuesday's outfit was covered in chili peppers, because, of course the Mexicans would appreciate that, an effort to bridge the language barrier.

Thursday's outfit was a little less breathable than the others but fashionable, covered in cowboy hats, boots, and lassos, because everyone knows Mexican children are suckers for Texans. It seemed my mother had found her calling. The Mexican sun had presented a sizzling challenge, and my mother had been up to the task—creating her own line of work clothes ensembles with a sizzle of their own!

At first I wasn't sure how I felt about these outfits. But Mom was walking around so proud of herself, calling me the cutest little chili pepper she had ever seen, that I wasn't sure that there was a way out. I mean, if we were going for unique or recognizable, we had undoubtedly reached our goal—something I supposed *could* be construed as positive. But then more and more, I saw other positive effects of wearing Mom's creations. Not only did it give her the motherly satisfaction of providing for her child, but her guerrilla warfare excuse was losing credibility. Because, really, what person, truly fearing the dangers of guerrilla warfare would deck their child in bright red chili peppers that scream, "Yes, I'm a privileged American; a product of a materialistic culture; a wannabe humanitarian! Come and get me!"

And so I neatly folded my cheap, cotton, sensible work outfits and placed them in my oversized duffle. I also packed my cute, manageable hammer, my work belt stuffed to the brim with disinfectant wipes, my work gloves (which were garden gloves adorned with ladybugs), my disposable camera, my modest one-piece bathing suit, enough sunscreen to blanket the hole in the ozone, my shower shoes, and my work boots. Add in too many toiletries, first aid, extra towels and sheets, an entire pharmacy of allergy meds, and every size and variety of Ziploc bags known to man, and there was no way in heaven *or* hell, for that matter, that I would be able to lift my giant duffle. So Mom reminded me of how "oh-so cute" I looked in my chili pepper outfit—her practiced, subtle way of suggesting that I remember to work it, modestly of course, and get some gullible church boy to carry my bag.

I was packed, I was ready, and I was well practiced in the getting-someone-else-to-carry-your-duffle mode of travel. All that was left was being dropped off at the church at *four in the morning*! By far, arriving *anywhere* at four in the morning was going to be the most difficult part of this trip. My mother, father, and I all said we could do it, while each of us secretly doubted success. Nonetheless—and surprisingly only 20 minutes late—my sleepy parents dropped their sleepy daughter off in the church parking lot that June 18th, 1995. This was by far the earliest any of us had ever been up for my birthday, and the situation wasn't likely to repeat itself. Without coffee, my mother managed only one final incoherent warning about guerrilla warfare: "Now April… safe…no guerrillas…drug lords…no warring." I imagine the youth pastor, Doug Edwards, made a joke about me selling drugs to guerrillas, which undoubtedly alarmed my mother and left her further dazed. Then with too many hugs, kisses, and a few "*Mooommm!*"s to end the hugging and kissing, I climbed into the church van and we were off.

I was 13. I was on my way to Mexico. I was 13. I was *on my way to Mexico*?!? *What the devil was I doing being 13 and going to Mexico*?????? I told myself to get a grip. "You are 13. You intend to go to Mexico. You are *supposed* to go to Mexico. And besides, you are 13 for goodness sake—*act your age*!" So with renewed confidence, I sat back in my seat, grinned, closed my eyes, and wondered about which outfit a 13-year-old ought to wear on her first day of work.

Finding

While I still remember my sensible, cotton work clothes, I have to admit, in all their flare, they are outshone in my memory by something—*Someone*—else. When I look back on that trip, I know that the girl who first set off for Mexico was not sure why she was going but only that something very strong and bigger than herself was taking her there. Amazingly, that same something did not leave her questions or curiosities unanswered once she arrived. No, He met her in Mexico, and in only a week's time, He sent a *very* different girl back home.

I've already told you that we left on my birthday. What I haven't told you is why that was so important to me when I was *almost* 13.

When I first started spending Monday nights with the church youth group, I stayed true to my mission: I made friends and met boys, but I paid little if any attention to the youth pastor's weekly message. Then something changed. My father was diagnosed with cancer, and my original mission on those Monday nights lost much of its meaning. Cancer came to live with us, and Death lurked at our backs. All of a sudden I began to listen to the messages. All of a sudden the messages were *very* important.

What happens when you die? …that question became a part of my daily thoughts and haunted my heart. I asked it for my father. Because he was sick, I thought much too much, at almost 13, about death and life, and life after death. For Dad, I begged the Unknown for answers. *Is God real*? I wondered. *Is heaven real*? And even more often, *is hell real*? Why would an almost-13-year-old be thinking about hell? Isn't that too dark for a girl so young? But it wasn't too dark, because in a very short amount of time it had occurred to me that my heart was dark, very dark, and very afraid.

So I listened. I said a prayer of salvation, as they called it, every time the youth pastor led us in one. I said those prayers every time—*because I wanted them to work*—but I didn't believe they would. Always, when the pastor began the prayer, I remembered the curse word I had said to a friend at school to sound cool, or the way I had yelled back at my father when he yelled at me. I could always come up with something sinful I had done, and so I said their prayer…and wished for it to work…and believed it wouldn't. In the back of my heart I felt the absence of true goodness: faith, hope and love. Sure, I knew my family loved me and I loved them, but I didn't hope in much; I didn't believe in much. And somehow, even at almost 13, I knew that the absence of hope and faith meant I didn't fully have love.

This was the condition of my life and my heart when one Monday night the youth pastor announced a mission trip to Mexico. I thought little of his announcement, until he told a story. Doug, the youth pastor, said that the church had taken a similar trip a few years ago with the youth and there had been a girl who wanted to go. She didn't have the money to go, and couldn't raise it. Still, the girl knew in her heart that she was supposed to go on this trip. One day Doug asked the girl why she felt so strongly she was supposed to go on this trip, and she answered that the group was leaving on her birthday. That departure date felt like fate to the young girl, and so, before her money was in, the church booked her ticket anyway. She waited for the money to come in, but it didn't. Then the day of their departure, her bags packed, she arrived at the church expectantly—still having not raised enough money to go on the trip. As she talked with Doug about what to do, someone approached them with a check. It had been left at the church office and was from no one the girl knew. Yet the check was for the exact amount of money she needed. Doug told us that if we were supposed to go on this trip to Mexico, God would find a way.

The exact dates of the trip had not been announced, so I didn't know that they were leaving on my birthday. Nonetheless, I thought a lot about that story over the next few weeks. What would it mean, I wondered, to have God make something happen for you? I didn't much believe in miracles anymore, yet I still dreamed of them; I still longed for the magical. Then, about two months before the group was leaving, the trip dates were announced. They were leaving on my birthday, and I couldn't help hoping, *just a little*, that maybe God was real; that maybe *this* was for me.

I told the youth pastor about the coincidence between the story and my circumstance, and he opted for the non-coincidental version. He told me he would help me get to Mexico. Then we both began trying to convince my parents to let me go. For a solid month the answer was not just a "No," but a "Hell No!" and I was at a loss. Then one day while my dad and I were riding in the car, I tried one last manipulative angle. But before I got to my most persuasive point, out of nowhere, he cut me off and said simply, "You can go if you keep your room clean for the next month." It was the strangest response. I was prepared to continue defending my reasons for going, but instead of finishing my argument, I just said, "Ok." Like that I was going to Mexico. We rode the rest of the way home in silence, both wondering what my mother was going to say and do to my father for making such an odd and consequential contract with me.

The rest of my getting to Mexico you know. You know that in half the time it took the other students I raised twice the money. You know about the pepper pants and the less breathable but fashionable Texas get-up. But you don't know what happened next.

Next is where it gets even stranger...*but better*.

We are in Mexico. We are working on a house

for an extremely poor family, and I am both disgusted and amazed.

I am disgusted by their living conditions. They live in the city dump, walking on 2 X 4's to cross the river of sewage running through the whole area. Their houses are not really houses, and they are always dirty, and everything always smells bad.

I am amazed, because the family for whom we are building this one room shack-of-a-house is always so happy. The matriarch of the family, the grandmother, is always smiling, with a look of peace and contentment in her eyes. The children are always laughing, and I am sure I have never sensed such joy and love in one place.

It makes me mad.

Of all the emotions I could have felt at the time, I was mostly furious. I was furious because their lives were terrible and yet they had more happiness and joy than I. I was also furious because the speaker at our camp each night kept talking about God breaking our hearts, and as a girl whose heart seemed continually in danger of breaking, God's wishes were not welcome. I was so mad deep inside, I did not know what to do with myself, and at the same time, I was falling in love with the Love that was all around me. It was intoxicating.

One night, toward the end of the week, our small church group was sitting by ourselves, outside, and Doug was talking. I have no idea what he was saying, because my mind was somewhere else. I was running everything back through my head: the whole week, the family's love and contentment, and my own restlessness and unhappiness. I was analyzing everything, dissecting each moment, doing what I always do.

Then, suddenly, it hit me.

Like a ton of bricks, I realized that the family, for whom we were building a one-room, un-air-conditioned, no-plumbing house in the middle of the city dump, *knew God*...**and that was enough.** They *knew* God! *that's* what made them happy! *that's* what gave them joy! I understood... something so small, and yet so important...and I wanted it for myself. So I silently said that "salvation prayer" I had said a hundred times, and for the first time I believed it would work. For the first time I knew it wasn't about me, what I had done or would do, but about Him, and what He had done and would do. I had found my constant; I had found my answer, and I finally knew why I had come to Mexico.

I remember having my eyes closed, praying these things, taking a leap of something new and unfamiliar, when the skeptic that is me recognized this new, unfamiliar something as *faith*—and immediately I had a moment of doubt. I remember I actually told God that if this was real, if *He* was real, I wanted Him to show me. I knew that the stars had not been out when I first closed my eyes, because the night was young and the sky was overcast. So being the silly dreamer-poet that I am, I asked God to fill the sky with stars. If He was real, I figured, He could do it. With one moment of pause and a deep breath I held just a moment too long, the girl who was barely 13 mentally crossed all her fingers and toes and dared to actually hope the impossible. I opened my eyes…and I've never—*before or since*—seen a more beautiful, sparkling sky.

Then I heard in my head, "April, you're going to be baptized." I looked at Doug, interrupting him completely, and I said, "Doug, I want to be baptized." He said, "OK," with a funny look on his face (after all, no one had been discussing baptism). Then two amazing days later, we flew home. Two days after that, I was baptized in a lake near my house, in front of my friends and my family. Several others from the trip were also baptized. In just eight days I had turned 13, I had met God, and I had been baptized with Him. Even I had underestimated what growing up, turning 13 and becoming a teenager, could really be.

... turning

Getting off the plane in Houston again and taking a school bus to a modest camp in Mexico (much different from the newly built camp in a border town in Texas the year before) would prove the least shocking experience of my second trip to Mexico. Our cabins were typical, small, quirky camp cabins, and our community bathrooms were typical, cramped, disgusting camp bathrooms. The boys in our group took to the setting immediately as the girls examined the situation thoroughly to see if anything could be done.

Realizing we girls had lucked out and gotten a cabin apart from the other girl groups, we put away our bags in our nice, secluded cabin, and for a moment things seemed to be looking up. But that soon changed. Coming back from checking out the below-par bathroom facilities, we were shocked to find girls we did not know, on their hands and knees—in the dirt, mind you—outside our cabin. Even more appalling was our discovery that they were trying to catch tarantulas to take back home with them. I do not know which part of this situation was the most unbelievable to us: (1) that a group of girls from Wisconsin could be strange and unfeminine enough to rejoice in such a discovery; (2)

that any group of girls existed in the world that could recognize a tarantula hole for what it was; or (3) that we were actually supposed to sleep in a cabin *surrounded by tarantulas*!!!! It was truly mind boggling, and we were at a loss for words. How were we supposed to make it through this mine field of poisonous treachery to even get to our stuff? I mean we had all hoped to freshen up a bit before dinner. But then looking at the display before us, we reasoned that in comparison to this present example of femininity and cleanliness, we were very likely to come out on top. With this mindset, and remembering the unfavorable bathroom conditions, we settled on exploring the rest of the camp, and of course, looking for boys. Maybe Wisconsin boys could outshine their female counterparts. As it turned out, they did. Soon we were less concerned about the tarantulas (*less* concerned, but still concerned).

As the week progressed, Robbie, a boy from Wisconsin, helped me discover a truth I had spent a year needing to find. On my first trip to Mexico I found real Love. Then for the next year, I tried to recapture that feeling at home. I tried to tell others what I had experienced. I tried to feel the same peace and contentment I had felt, if only for a moment. But it wasn't always easy. And so I had come back to Mexico, a year later, to find that feeling again. Almost the moment I stepped foot on the worksite, it was back. I was full of joy, hope, love, faith. I was on top of the world. Robbie, who had grown up in the church, who had discovered this great Love somewhere far from Mexico, had come here now to rekindle that joy, hope, love, and faith—and he saw it in me. He in turn made me realize that you didn't always have to come to Mexico to find it. If he, and so many in his group, had felt those things before, in other places, at home with their families, then it was *possible*. By the end of the week, God had shown me that it wasn't about *where* you were, it was about *Who* was with you.

When I left Mexico, I took God home, just as I had the year before, but this time I understood what that actually meant. Robbie and I kept in touch for years, and he was always a reminder of that very important lesson. For a year in my life—when I was 13—I thought I had found and left a home for my heart in the strangest of all places, in Mexico. Then when I was 14, I found that my home was with Him, and He was everywhere, and He would never leave me. With His help, since that second trip to Mexico I have survived much more than tarantulas.

CANCER

The History of our Cancer

I was eleven when Dad was first diagnosed. My dad has cancer? *My dad*? But my dad lifts weights; my dad does pushups; my dad couldn't have cancer. Unfortunately, the cancer wasn't discouraged by my protests. Some things are bigger than we are. They are bigger than our plans, and they are out of our control. We learned quickly that cancer was one of them.

Over five years we were told three times that my father had less than a year to live. By the third time, the news had become strangely familiar.

It began as a malignant lymphoma in Dad's shoulder. They removed it. They gave him chemo. They treated it with radiation. Two and a half years later it came back.

This time it was in his jaw. More chemo. More radiation. His tongue was burned, bleeding, and swollen. He was always nauseated. We watched, helpless, as his appetite diminished and eating became a painful duty. Still *somehow*, my father ate.

So many of these simple pleasures, the everyday small things we had taken for granted, were slipping away, like his hair. His dark brown hair, that I used to play *Sports Bar Barbershop* with as a child, had long since become only a memory. It had fallen out the first time, and it fell out the second time, too. It started with just pieces, but those pieces became clumps. He even lost the hair on his arms and legs. He didn't want to wait for it all to fall out—to watch it happen so slowly—so our hairdresser, and longtime friend of my father's, told him to come in and she'd shave it all off for free. That way he felt he still had some control. That way he felt he still had some power of choice left in it all.

She never charged him for a haircut after that. When he had enough hair to come in and get it trimmed, payment was never mentioned. Since the occasion was so rare, it became a kind of celebration. You learned to revel in the small victories, and everyone silently rejoiced with us. Whenever his hair did grow back in, it sometimes had a curl to it that had never been there before. The color was even different, and the texture followed suit. But like so much else, we no longer tried to make sense of these things. No one can make sense of these things.

After his second round of treatments, they told us that they thought they had gotten what was in his jaw. I distinctly noticed the "all" to be missing. Last time they told us they thought they had gotten it *all*...meaning *everywhere*. Now, the "all" had been replaced by a murmur about something in his bone marrow. Around hospital corners and in the looks doctors exchanged, there were whispers of an unknown culprit, a lurking predator that their supposedly able arms of knowledge and advanced methods had not yet reached.

And so they ran more tests...and still more tests...until I believed tests would never give us answers. They had doctor powwows, and they tried to draw firm conclusions that could help them formulate a plan of attack. But I knew who they were looking for. No test would ever name him, but I had sensed his presence ever since that very first night when cancer came to live with us. Death was the culprit. Death—with his poisonous fingers that groped and assaulted my father—was turning Dad's own body against him.

"It's low-grade cancer," they finally told us. "It won't grow quickly," they said, "but it will resist the chemo better than any of the faster growing kinds we have treated in Ted before." We all felt so defeated. I felt so much hate. "*Why is this happening?*" my heart was shouting. "What the hell do you mean your hands are tied? Well untie them, then! DO SOMETHING! *Fix* my father!"

But they were out of tests. We were almost out of options. "There is one more possibility..." they began. "A last resort..." "We wouldn't suggest it if there was another way..." "You don't have to go through with it..." **"But I think we should start looking for a bone marrow donor."**

And there it was: We had to decide if we would take the chance on a transplant. Even if we didn't find a donor, they told us, they recommended a stem cell transplant. It was an experimental procedure which essentially emptied my father of his bone marrow as a transplant would, and then put his good bone marrow back into his body. Everything was just like a transplant, except that the donor would be my father.

So these were our options. The odds were not good with either of these procedures. The doctors still didn't have it down to a perfect science. There was a good chance he would die from the procedure, but there was a 100 percent chance he would die without it. Is that really a question then? Is that really a choice? For my family, it wasn't, but I understand now, after the fact, why it is for so many, why it might be for me now.

Transplanted Dreams

People can never be the same after one of these transplants. Your body never fully recovers. There has been too much trauma; it has borne too much. The same is true with your heart.

You've been holding your breath, standing on the slope of a mountain waiting for an avalanche that may never come, that could come any second, but either way you feel sure you'll never stop waiting for it. You forgot how to breathe normally. After so much time on the edge, is there a normal, a flat land where one can wisely return? I wasn't sure then, but I suppose I could give an answer pretty easily now.

No. The answer is no. There is no lasting flat land, no unstained reality, no uneventful normal where one can return. Eventually you learn there never was. Instead your eyes were simply closed and your feet kept steady by the unknown. Then, when life finally does settle down, and simple, nonsensical joys begin to rejoin your world, you will never actually trust them. You won't count on those moments.

Don't get me wrong: you will enjoy them, but you will also know that they are not meant to last forever. Moments, circumstances, by their very nature are meant to pass, and faith is made perfect only when placed in other things. What kind of things? Eternal things. The Eternal thing. Nothing else lasts.

I guess, more than anything, He is what I learned best. He is what I came away with. From Mexico, from cancer, from a little town in central Florida to a big world: He is what I came away with, and in this most important way my heart was changed forever. From such a point, from such a change, there is no turning back.

But that is OK. That is real. And I learned quickly, that forward is hard enough; there's just no sense in trying to turn back time.

MOMENTUM

Strength

Strength is such a deceptive intangible. I've been watching the 2008 Olympics over the past few days, and I've seen amazing strength. As I've watched the games, I've thought that the Olympians' bodies resemble Italian marble statues much more than human beings, and I've admired them. Their sweat and hard work is inspiring and incredible, and in their amazing stature and strength we all see a hint of what humanity could be. We all celebrate this hint of perfection.

Yet even in the Olympics perfect strength is elusive. A world watches as its best and brightest athletes reach headlong for that perfection...and we all hold our breaths as even gold medalists seem to miss it by just inches. This Olympics has been the first where the Perfect 10 in gymnastics no longer exists. But I remember when it did exist. I remember a rare Perfect 10 routine being followed by a less-than-10 routine. I remember a Perfect 10 routine being scrutinized by announcers watching the slow motion instant replay. I remember Perfect 10s as fleeting, unrepeatable, yet still glorious moments in time: solidarity which is somehow slightly less perfect for being so fleeting. Slightly less perfect, yet still majestic and awe-inspiring.

For myself, I've experienced in my own life very

different types of strength. I am not, by any means an athlete. In fact, I am so far from being an athlete that the concept is laughable; hilarious even for those who know me best. What I have always had, however, is inner strength; a fighting spirit. What I haven't always understood about my strength is that even the inner strength which the mind wills into being cannot maintain itself forever. It too will run out. It too will miss perfection by inches. It too will at some point fail.

The night my father first told me of his cancer, I watched his and my mother's strength fail. I watched, and I vowed to be strong. I vowed to be strength perfected, and for almost five years, I did not break this vow I had made to myself. Naively, over time, I thought I had mastered inner strength. Naively, I began to believe I was strong. I forgot that Perfect 10s are always followed by 9-point-somethings. I forgot that sometimes, when Death is lurking, a perfect performance of strength has no follow-up routine. I did not fathom then what I would need to know, when the routine of strength is over and the hint of perfection is gone. I never imagined how a broken athlete who has missed by inches, who has missed by feet, who is surrounded by dreams that will now never come true ... gets up. I did not know I needed to think through such a simple action. I did not know I wouldn't know how.

Grace

The summer I turned 16 was sweet for a moment. That moment lasted for three days in Butte, Montana. As I've already told you, my family took vacations out west when I was growing up. My father had family in Montana, and we sometimes visited them along our way. This trip was like that, and my parents and I were scheduled to visit relatives in Butte at the very end of our trip.

But before we got to Butte, many other things happened. Most of my extended family came to visit us on vacation. My mother's brother Neil, his wife, Marta, and their two children, my cousins Sean and Cristina, came from Florida. Their visit overlapped ever so slightly with the visit of my father's family. His older brother Chuck came from Washington D.C. Uncle Chuck's two sons, my cousins Greg and Bryan also came. My mother's parents, my Nana and Honey, were supposed to come, and their absence was strongly felt and not discussed. All these loved ones came, and while it was exciting to be with them, it was difficult to ignore the "Why?" of their coming. They came, because they knew this might be their last chance to spend time with my Dad in the place where even he felt like cancer couldn't touch him. They came to take in through his eyes the majesty of the mountains he loved. They came for him.

Such knowledge was a lot for my newly 16-year-old mind to process. So I didn't. I was still imagining my strength wouldn't run out. I was still imagining the end would not come.

The fall of 1995, when I was 13, after two different battles with various cancers, my dad underwent a stem cell transplant. He spent 23 days in an isolated unit where even greeting cards had to be sanitized, his water cost hundreds of dollars, and I had to put on an entire sanitized suit just to see him. He almost lost his mind in those 23 days. He endured incredible pain as they gave him the maximum amount of chemo a body can take so that his body couldn't fight the procedure. He was going stir crazy from the isolation, and he apparently threatened suicide more than once. Some of the nurses were a little frightened by him, and well, I was just frightened. But he made it through. And then to the nurses' relief, he moved over to the double-wide.

He could not come home, because I was in school and constantly surrounded by germs. Plus we had a dog, and the combination of these circumstances made our house a danger zone and not an option. A retired friend of the family volunteered to go live with him in a mobile home near the hospital and take care of him. He had to stay there for months, and we didn't see him enough, because the hospital was almost two hours away.

But finally he did come home, and for a long time we all thought we had made it through. We pretended remission really was the equivalent of cured, and for a while we moved on with our lives.

Until something changed. Dad wasn't feeling so well again, but no one would say why. Everyone feared what it might be, and it wasn't long before my immediate, and much of my extended family, found themselves with us once more in Montana, reaching out for a piece of something good and normal; something we could all remember.

While I did take note of the underlying reality of our little family vacation (because my analytical mind has never been able to ignore such things), I only took note of it. I did not process it further. I did nothing else with it.

And then we came to Butte. Our extended, non-Montana family was gone, and we had just one stop left before my parents and I flew home. I wasn't looking forward to it. If you've ever been to Butte… well, there just isn't much there. It is a strip mining town and it has been stripped thoroughly. But when we arrived in Butte, I knew I was feeling something which had seemed lost for quite some time: I was happy.

Our first day in Butte, we met up with some of my dad's second cousins. After the "oh-my-how-she-has-grown's" were over, it was decided that I would be taken to a baseball game in which my 18-year-old third cousin, Stephen, was playing. The plan was that after the game, I would be deserted by my parents and left to hang out with a cousin I had never met, and his 18-year-old friends.

At first I was skeptical. But then I met Stephen, and his disarming smile and friendly demeanor put me immediately at ease. In about an hour's time, I genuinely felt like I had known Stephen my whole life. It was strange, actually, but for a girl who hadn't emotionally relaxed in five years, being with someone who didn't know her story, someone who felt like a true kindred spirit, whatever that expression really means...well, it was such an awesome kind of refreshing, I simply didn't question it. From that point on, I spent every waking second with Stephen and his friends. After the first day, it occurred to me that my parents had originally planned on staying only a day in Butte, allowing us to make a slow trek, with a couple of stops, back to the airport in Denver. But instead of leaving the next morning, we stayed. It wasn't discussed, but we stayed, and I knew my parents recognized a light in my eyes they had both been missing. They saw it here in Butte, Montana, of all places, and so we stayed in Butte as long as we could.

What did Stephen and I do for three days? For me, I suppose it felt like we crammed several carefree teenage summers into just three days. We went boating on his friend's boat. We went swimming in a glacier lake that was much too cold. We saw the movie Armageddon which had just come out in the theatres, and I actually allowed myself to openly cry when Bruce Willis's character dies to save his daughter. One night we drove up a mountain to a lookout point, and Stephen, his friend Dan and I sat in lawn chairs and talked about life. The lights of Butte sparkled from up that high, and I was encouraged that even a strip-mining town with little beauty in the daylight was renewed from that vantage point.

Dan spent most of those three days with us, and he too felt like a dear friend I had known forever. Before I left he gave me a baseball cap he had been breaking in for the three days I was there, and although it might seem silly, I have kept that hat all these years. It serves as a reminder of a brief but wonderful moment in my adolescence where I was simply 16, and the world was almost innocent.

What did we talk about for those three days? What didn't we talk about? The whole world seemed before us, and it felt like we covered it all. ...God. Love. Heartache. Dreams. Hope. Faith. Stephen said my coming to Butte was like a reawakening for him. He was about to leave home for college, and he realized it was time to rethink his trajectory, and remember what mattered. For me, my coming to Butte was the calm before the storm, and there is simply no better way to put it. I penned that phrase in my journal the day I left, because I knew the calm was what I had just experienced, and I knew that the storm would soon follow. I had been watching storms roll in my whole life, and I knew how to spot them. This, however, was the first storm I didn't want to experience.

But I wasn't experiencing it yet. I knew in every part of me that God had handed me three perfect days to be 16 years old: no pain, no fears, just happy. What probably surprised me most about the experience was how fully and without hesitation I embraced it. The girl who had guarded the wall around her heart for so long, and with such vigilance, allowed herself to exhale. I let myself be unguarded for three whole days. I let myself recognize the ringing of unhindered laughter as it escaped me. I let myself hope, and dream, and forgot to worry about coming down off that high. I forgot to fear the bottom; I didn't avoid the high to save myself the pain of the low. I very simply accepted God's gift and didn't think about the consequences until they were falling all around me as we drove to Denver.

Even now, I am amazed at the grace that surrounded that experience. God did not owe me calm before the storm. I had smelled rain in the air around me for five years, and God did not have to bring three days of sunshine before the sky gave way to black.

But He did.

He did, because He truly does always bring the sun. To me that phrase "He Brings the Sun" means that He always brings you out of darkness. There is always a new dawn and another side to every dark night, every storm, and He is always there waiting. But that same phrase also means to me that His grace is often more than salvation in the end. Sometimes His grace saves you in the middle. Sometimes His grace is beauty in the midst of a personal hell. His grace is so much more than sufficient. His grace IS perfection, and when it comes to His brand of gifts, perfection does not miss by inches. His perfection has an eternal endurance. And this is a precious truth: because He will endure *for* you.

R a i n

It rained most of the drive from Butte to Denver. It rained, and I cried—staring out the window and seeing nothing. I no longer seemed to have the strength or the will left to stop the tears. I did keep them silent most of the drive, but my parents knew I was crying. They knew and they let me be.

I clutched my journal and wrote in it intermittently. The storm was coming, the edges were already here. I could feel it in my heart, and I could see it as huge raindrops hit the outside of my backseat window. I realized for the first time, that I was not ready for it. All that preparation, all the holding it together and being the strong one seemed now like wasted time. I wasn't ready. And the dread felt overwhelming; suffocating.

At some point we boarded a plane and landed in Florida. We were no longer 'not talking' about why Nana and Honey had not joined us on vacation. We were still not talking about how sick my dad really was, but we were talking about Honey, my beloved grandfather.

Honey had been diabetic since he was 17. Long before I could remember, he had lost the feeling in his feet and calves due to the diabetes. Just before our trip, he and my Nana had been walking around a construction site, looking at the floor plan of a house. He stepped on a nail that went through his shoe and into his foot, but he did not discover it until later that night. Not until he was undressing before bed did he realize what had happened. While we were away out west he spent most of his time with doctors. He had little to no circulation running through that part of his legs, and the wound was not healing. The outlook was terribly uncertain.

Although we were finally home and getting the truth, I was due to leave again on my third trip to Mexico with the youth group in just a few days. Now I didn't know if I wanted to go. My grandfather, however, wanted me to go. He had always been the one who most of all supported my involvement with the youth group. This time, however, my parents also wanted me to take the trip. Everyone seemed to think it would be best, be good for me even, but I wasn't so sure. It felt wrong to be leaving. It felt a bit like cheating, but with their continual urgings and reassurances I finally decided I would go.

I don't remember that trip the way I remember the others. I simply remember being afraid. I remember being unable to call and speak with my family for the four or five days we were in Mexico. I remember continually trying to swallow the lump in my throat that told me things were not OK at home. People can hug you and tell you everything will be OK—and they did—but that doesn't reassure a girl who has learned that God's promise to love us and never leave us is not a promise to spare us from the realities of life and death. He doesn't shield us from pain, He simply never leaves our side and He shoulders what we cannot. Sometimes this means He shoulders us when we cannot carry ourselves. His love does heal, but those who need healing, first have been broken.

I have only one distinct and vivid memory from that third trip to Mexico. It was the 4th of July, and we were in San Diego, planning to cross the border the following day. It was nighttime, and we had gone down to the pier hoping to see fireworks. Our youth pastor, Doug, asked the group to crowd around me and Scott, another student, because both of us had left some uncertainty at home. The group crowded in close, laying their hands on us if they could reach us, or touching the person beside them if they couldn't. Then they prayed for us, and I let my tears flow out silently. Every time I felt that foreign wetness in my eyes I was a little shocked. This was the very reaction and emotion I had avoided so successfully for so long, but here I was again, leaking.

My closest friend, Beth, had her hand on my back. And I felt much comfort in that. Beth was as much a part of my family as anyone. She loved Honey and my father, and I knew she was feeling this with me. Then, as she prayed out loud for me, what sounded like fireworks began. There was a symphony playing in an open amphitheatre just a little ways down the water's edge, and the fireworks sounded like percussion to the music. I remember feeling each loud explosive boom in my chest, and the feeling was unmistakable. It felt like hope breaking through. It felt as if Beth's words were invading my despair, flowing through her hand on my back with each explosion. When she finished and we all opened our eyes, I turned around and asked her in bewilderment, "Did you feel that?" She smiled and nodded her head with soft happiness. We hugged and turned to see the fireworks we had been feeling. But there were no fireworks. The noise we had heard and felt was the sound of canons being fired by the symphony for their grand finale. We saw no fireworks that evening.

California, like Florida, had been experiencing a drought that summer, and that part of the July 4th celebration had been cancelled. So we listened to the music, I practiced breathing as I had become accustomed to doing, and then we all headed back to the hotel to rest before setting out for Mexico in the morning.

Like that I blinked, and the trip was over. Suddenly I was in the San Diego airport and on my way home. When I got to Florida, it was raining again, and this did not surprise me. In fact, I half expected to see rain when I got off the plane. Both my parents came to pick me up from the airport, and to my dismay they announced that we were driving straight to the hospital, where they had already spent the past few hours. As we drove, my parents told me that Honey was not doing well, that he was already in surgery. When we got there we could only wait. Some of us sat, but many of us paced. My Uncle Neil, Aunt Marta, Sean and Cristina were there. The faces of some of my family had the blank, soul-less expressions of those who do not know what they should be thinking and so instead abandon the present moment all together.

Then the doctor came in. Honey was stable for the present. The wound in his foot had reached the point of last resort, and they had amputated his leg.

No outcome could have been more upsetting to me. I suppose you would have to have known my Honey to understand my reaction. I knew I should be happy that maybe the doctors had found a way to save him, but I couldn't bear the thought of my Honey's face looking down where his leg had once been. My grandfather was a proud man. Maybe I should see that as a fault, but, with him, I didn't; I still don't. It was one of the many reasons I loved him. He was the quintessential Southern gentleman, the perfect combination of Cary Grant and a Georgia farmer (even though in real life he'd been an accountant). He was an incredibly hard worker, sweating for and earning everything he had. He was the greatest story teller I've ever known, spinning fanciful tales with mischief and love in his blue-grey eyes. He was always impeccably dressed and had impeccable taste. But above all, my grandfather commanded my respect. He did this without force or fear; he very simply had a presence about him. He had taught my cousins and I to do everything with our heads held high, and in many ways, it was his favor that we each sought most. He gave it readily, but to lose it was worse than any punishment our parents could inflict. We loved him. Deeply. There is just no other way to say it.

Yet here, in this unremarkable hospital bed lay my mangled hero. He smiled at us. I didn't smile back. I was not ready for this. Whatever happened next could not happen next. I wouldn't survive it. Honey took my hand and gave me a very meaningful look that said "I believe in you—always have." I squeezed his hand back.

Another church trip was coming up in only a few days. It was summer, and most of the youth trips were crammed into that season. This trip was a small thing. Only a few student leaders and staff were going to the beach for the weekend for some much needed reflection time. I said I wasn't going, but then Honey asked me to go anyway—and he was insistent about it. I think it was his way of giving me one last gift. He knew too well what I knew and what everyone else seemed to be denying: Dad didn't have much time left. He knew that heartache was coming for me soon, and he knew he could not spare me from it. So instead, he asked me to leave him for a few days and escape from the all-too-familiar hospital.

I hate hospitals. If you spent much of your childhood waiting in one—always waiting—you would hate them, too. They smell. They make me claustrophobic. The hallways and doorways reek of death. I hate hospitals, and Honey knew this. He hated them for me. He also loved his son-in-law very much, and he had spent much time in hospitals as well, waiting on Dad. All of us had done so much waiting. Over the years of Dad's many treatments, I had stayed with my grandparents so much that it became my routine to spend the weekend nights there. In many ways, Honey was a second father to me.

So now I listened to him. I felt the choking in my throat, the distinct dread of something coming that I could not stop and I felt sure I could not handle. It was coming with such force and speed that I wanted desperately to break into a run and not look back. Instead, I decided to go with my church group to the beach as Honey had pleaded with me to do. Everyone said that Honey would be here when I got back and this would be good for me, and all of those things people tell you. Honey didn't say that. He and I knew better than to assume things we could not know.

While I have never believed people when they say these things, I have always smiled and nodded and pretended to believe for their sake. People cling to the façade of those words like they are life itself, and I always knew the least I could do was keep the façade intact for them a little bit longer. Sure, denial can be one's worst enemy, but everyone copes differently with tragedy, and who am I to judge the fragile threads that hold hearts so delicately together? So I smiled and nodded and hugged my desperate, fragile family, and then when everyone had left Honey's hospital room, I pretended to have left something behind and turned back. I stood there at the foot of his bed for several moments, taking him in. Then I rushed over, hugged him fiercely, told him I loved him, told him goodbye, and left the room running until I caught up to my family. Somewhere in me I knew I would not see him again. I left for the beach and waited for the phone call I knew would come.

Hope

You may judge me harshly for leaving. I'm OK with that, and I even understand it. But Honey didn't judge me. I was spared watching Pleny DuPree, my Honey, my hero, fade into the weak, horrible humility that precedes death. I would see it soon enough, but at least my grandfather could always stand tall in my heart and memories.

The call did come while we were at the beach. It came, and for the rest of the day I sat in a hotel conference room with my small group, rocking myself in a chair, leaking tears silently for the most part. It really was the best place I could have been. I looked as if I did not want to be touched, and so mostly no one touched me. They just let me rock and leak. At times they prayed for me, but they just let me hurt in my own way. I was given my space but I wasn't alone, and that was exactly what my barely-together heart needed at that moment. One of the leaders, Jason, also a close family friend, gave me a leather cross necklace. I remember rubbing my fingers over it monotonously as I rocked.

Beth was there. And that night we walked along the beach, meaning to talk, but mostly just walking. She was always good like that. She never pushed.... Then suddenly we heard it. That same boom we had heard on the shore in San Diego. She grabbed my shoulder and we exchanged a meaningful look. Then we turned around to see the fireworks exploding over the Daytona pier. Holding hands we ran back over to the group, toward the fireworks to watch them. No one in Florida had seen fireworks all summer, but with all the rain my little storm had brought, they were finally setting some off here at the beach. And there it was again. That God who never leaves was reminding me that He was there. That God who doesn't always shield us from the pain was reminding me that His brand of Hope cannot be outdone—not even by Death.

Hope Floats is one of my favorite movies, and the line that gives the movie its title is more spot-on than most things people say and the advice they give to those in heartache. Time does not heal all wounds, and things won't always be OK. But..."Just give hope a chance to float up. And it will, too" (Sandra Bullock in Hope Floats). Just before that line in the movie, Sandra Bullock says, "Childhood is what you spend the rest of your life trying to overcome. That's what Momma always says. She says that beginnings are scary, endings are usually sad, but it's the middle that counts the most." This is true. The middle does count the most.

I've found that the middle is actually the hardest. In the middle we can clothe ourselves with false strength. In the middle we forget how much we need help. In the middle we cannot always see ourselves. We see ourselves more clearly through the wetness of humility brought by the scariness of beginnings and the pain of endings. I've needed salvation in the middle, the beginning, and the end. So thankfully for us all, the God I know is Lord over all three.

A Rainbow

We had a memorial service at home, but the funeral was in Georgia where Honey was buried with the rest of his family. They made an exception for me at the viewing in Georgia. I did not want to see him lying there, lifeless and unfamiliar. He had spared me watching life leave him, and I never wanted a mental picture of him without warmth in his skin and life in his eyes. So they opened and closed the casket, depending on when I entered and left the room. I had planned on staying out of the room altogether, but my family wouldn't have it. They arranged it with the funeral director, who managed it quietly and seamlessly, though I imagine it seemed strange to those who were not immediate relatives.

Dad and I had to leave early. As soon as the graveside service ended we started for home. Everyone else was staying a few days, but school was starting for me, and I had a year of pre-calculus and trigonometry to teach myself before that first day. I had made a deal with my calculus teacher that I could skip those two courses, if I could prove to her satisfaction that I had the background to go on into calculus without them. With all that had been going on, and because I am a horrible procrastinator, I had waited to begin study until just days before the start of school. But it was really the perfect situation. It gave me something to do that required the majority of my brain power, and by now, I welcomed distractions of all kinds.

As Dad and I drove, not speaking, both thinking, the rain that had seemed to pour down for weeks stopped. Just like that the sky became brightly sunny, and a double rainbow arched across the entire horizon. It was hugely uplifting for my dad and me, and we marveled at it. A bit dumbfounded by the clear sky, I said simply, "The rain stopped." Dad gave a weak smile, as if he knew just what I meant, and understood why I said those words with such doubt and mistrust. He replied, "I guess it has."

For a moment there in the car, hope floated up beautifully again for a broken father and daughter.

Aloud

Over the next couple of months, Dad got sicker. Finally we said aloud what I had known for a while: the cancer was back. Mom told me the news, officially, when I was at Beth's house one night. Beth and I were getting ready for the girls' choice Sadie Hawkins Dance, and I had asked one of my closest guy friends, Ryan Wilson, to be my date. I was counting on the night being easy, uneventful fun where no one would ask me how my life was really going. One of the hardest parts about all we were going through was how publically my mother and I had to grieve. Both of my parents were longtime teachers at my high school, and my dad had coached various sports. Everyone knew my family. My friends either knew my dad through me or because he had taught or coached them. So I felt that everyone was watching me as my father faded. Maybe they really didn't watch me, but it always felt that way.

There at Beth's house, we were almost finished getting ready for the dance. I was putting on mascara, which I rarely wore, when Mom arrived. She wasn't supposed to come to Beth's house and Dad had gone to a doctor's appointment that day, so I knew her arrival wasn't a good thing. She came in Beth's room and Beth immediately left as her mother motioned silently for her to come out. Mom sat on the bed behind me, and I stayed standing at the dresser, looking at her through the mirror. I was giving off my "don't touch me" bristled vibe, and so my mother didn't. She apologized for telling me before the dance, but she thought I'd want to know that the doctors had told us today that they expected my Dad would have only three months. Her voice cracked a little at the end of her words. I remained motionless, staring at her through the mirror. I gritted my teeth together and silently told myself that I would not cry. I had already done my makeup. As heartless as that sounds, it wasn't. It was just as much emotion as I could spare at the moment without falling to pieces. I wasn't ready to fall to pieces. Not yet. Mom saw that I wasn't going to move, and she understood that my slight nod meant both that I understood and that I had expected what she was telling me. And then she simply left. Beth came back in and squeezed my shoulder. I said, "I don't want to talk about it." And she said, "OK."

Either Ryan picked me up, or I him, I don't really remember, but then we were off to the dance. I guess he must have driven after all, because I remember sitting in the passenger's seat with my head tilted back blinking profusely to avoid any tears that threatened my composure and my makeup. Head tilted back, I told him, "We just found out my Dad has three months. I don't want to talk about it. I don't want to cry, and I want to have fun tonight." There was a silent pause. I stopped blinking, took a breath and looked at Ryan. "OK?" I asked. “Sure thing,” he said. He was always the class clown, so he probably tried to make me laugh that night, but I don’t remember if it worked.

Conversations

It wasn't three months.

Over the next three weeks, my dad and I talked a lot about God and faith and heaven. Maybe these conversations began before we got the news, but I can't remember. So much of that summer and fall is a blur in my mind. But I do know that it was suffocatingly pressing and important to both of us to discuss these things. Dad could no longer see well enough to read, and his pain was so great that he could bear to stay awake and talk only for very short bursts. So I read to him. He asked me to read the Bible to him, and I did. He asked me how I had survived this so far, and I told him. He asked me if I would be OK, and I lied. Yet a part of me knew it wasn't fully a lie, because God would survive this, He would remain constant when I became useless, and He would not leave. There had to be hope in that, I figured.

I read my favorite Psalm to Dad, the one that told me God was constant. Over and over I repeated one verse, Psalm 139:18, "When I awake, I am still with You." I clung to that verse, and I begged my father to cling to it as well.

He wanted to, but he couldn't.

He kept telling me that he desperately wanted to have the confidence that I had that Jesus really was the Son of God. He wanted to believe that Jesus had died for his sins as well as mine and the whole world's. He wanted to believe that when Jesus rose from the dead He conquered death and that mere belief in what He had accomplished through His death and resurrection would save us all from ourselves. He wanted to know that Jesus really was "The Way the Truth and the Life, and [that] no one comes to the Father but through [Him]," (John 14:6) but he just didn't know it. Deep in his heart he felt the same doubt his so-like-him, skeptical daughter had struggled against at age 13. I told him that the doubt doesn't go away until you make that leap of faith. But he couldn't jump.

More than anything he shared with me during those conversations, I remember one sentiment. He told me one day that if he could dare ask God, he would want only to be a servant in someone else's heavenly mansion. To clean the golden floors of Mother Teresa's well-earned heavenly home, he thought would be amazing. This broke my heart, and humbled me greatly. My father was always more humble than me. He was more aware of his sin and weakness that anyone I ever knew. It hindered him in a lot of ways, but at least pride was not his problem. Yet his humbleness broke my heart because while he understood he didn't deserve God's grace, he had failed to understand that neither did Mother Teresa. No one deserves it. Even those who come close to what we think is perfection still miss it. Worldly perfection is fleeting. It is but a shadow of His perfect love. And whether you miss by inches or miles…you miss. THAT is grace. "But many who are first will be last, and the last first" (Matthew 19:30). But my father could not grasp that a mansion could be his.

So many things were stacked against us. One day I came home to find Dad in a lawn chair on our front porch. He was sitting like he always did when we watched together as storms rolled in. This day it was sunny, however, and a different storm glared at us from the horizon. He had been crying—something I was still not used to. Besides when he was first given the news that he had cancer and then here at the end, my dad had been pretty good about shielding his pain from me. When I would drive with him to Shands (the teaching hospital where he was treated) for the bone marrow biopsies he seemed to always need during those five years, Dad never accepted sedatives. Instead, he bit down on a towel while Kate, his nurse, drilled a hole in his hip bone. Kate was privy to a lot of curse words from my father, but he never would take the meds. He wanted to be awake and able to fake health on his drive back with me. I doubt he realized I knew what it cost him. He didn't want me to know, so I pretended I didn't.

But here he was today, unabashedly in tears, and I didn't know what to do. I didn't have to come up with something, however, because almost immediately he just started talking. "I wanted to see you graduate," he started. "I wanted to walk you down the aisle. I wanted to see it all." There was a pause. I had tears in my eyes now, too. "I'm so sorry…" he said, and then he could no longer speak.

"I know, Dad, I know, but it's not your fault. It's nobody's fault."

A few days later in the car he asked me, "How can you not blame God?" It was an abrupt question that came without warning. Strangely, however, I found that I was ready for it. I had thought about it before. "I can't," I told him, "because I need Him too much." He nodded.

* * * * * * *

My account of this next conversation is out of sequence. I don't know when we had it, but I think it was before we got the news. Dad was dropping me off at Vicki's house one night for girls' discipleship. Just before I got out of the car, he told me, "I bought two cemetery plots today. One for me and one for your Mom one day. They are near Grandma's grave." I was caught completely off guard. I looked at him. I have no idea what my expression looked like, but I simply nodded and got out of the car.

That night, among my peers and leaders there was some of that same rocking and silent leaking there had been when Honey died.

Another afternoon Dad went over some of his funeral arrangements with me. It might sound cruel or odd for a father to do this with his 16-year-old daughter, but it wasn't. My Mom is a much more fragile creature, in some ways, than I. Although she has more strength than she has ever realized. Still, my Mom is one who needs her denial as long as it will last her. Maybe that is why I am sensitive to that kind of coping, but I truly believe that we are all stitched up in different ways. The stitching is fragile in every one of us, and it takes a lot of grace to keep us together. I figure the crutches we choose are our own business, and I never questioned mine or my mother's. But from my father's perspective, I was the one constantly bringing up the topic of death and heaven and other heavy matters when it was just Dad and me. Mom didn't bring up these things, so I suppose in a sense I had opened the door and he had little choice but to walk through it.

* * * * * * *

In so many ways, I grew up that fall. I went from being 16 to miniature adult, overnight. I do not regret this lack of transition, however, because I know I am who I am because of it. I know the lessons I came away with are steadier in some ways than years of practice. I suppose I cannot change it, so I do not wish I could.

Knowing

About 5:30 in the morning Mom woke me up. "April, wake up! Wake up! It's your Dad. You have to help me!" Instantly, I was wide awake. We ran back to their bedroom where Dad was mumbling incoherent nonsense as the morphine often made him do. He was lying on the floor. "What happened?" I blinked out. "I think he tried to get up to go to the bathroom in the middle of the night, but he fell." He had soiled himself, and was so upset and discombobulated that he was fighting my mother as she tried to lift him.

Together my mother and I wrestled him back onto the bed. There was nothing else for either of us to say. Mom gave me a horrified look, and told me that I should get ready for school.

I did. I went to school. It was a Monday.

Then I came home.

There were way too many cars in my driveway. I had a brief panic attack thinking for just a moment that my dad had died and no one had told me. But then I realized that would never happen, so I parked the car and got out. I went to the front door, and Uncle Neil opened it for me. I stared at him. He lived five hours away. He hugged me, and I immediately went looking for Mom. There were SO MANY people there, and everyone wanted to hug me or pat my shoulder or make some kind of contact that I didn't want made. It wasn't their fault, but all I could think was, where is Mom, and what is going on???

I eventually found her. She said she had called hospice after what happened that morning. It had only been three weeks since we got the news, but we both knew now that we weren't going to get our full three months.

I didn't go to school Tuesday. The throngs of people didn't leave either. Half the time I found myself consoling others, instead of them consoling me, but I preferred it that way: It kept me busy, and I felt less vulnerable. Sometime on Tuesday, Dad came to and seemed to be with it, so everyone cleared out of my parent's bedroom where the hospital bed had been set up. My mom and I then went in for our final goodbyes.

This time we all cried. Dad apologized over and over for not being the husband and dad he thought he should have been; that he had wanted to be. We told him to stop saying such things. We told him we loved him. Then he looked me straight in the eye squeezed my hand and said with fierce intensity, "I Know." No words I had ever heard were as beautiful as those words to me. My father had decided to make a leap of faith, and he had found hope, love, and faith on the other side. He finally knew—a phrase we had discussed so many times—that God was real and Jesus was the only way. Those are the last coherent words my father ever said to my mother or me.

That Tuesday night, just before midnight, Dad breathed his last breath. This time everyone was in the room. I was crammed between the far wall and Dad's bed, holding his hand. When it was over, I remember my dad's oldest brother, Chuck, closing Dad's eyes. Uncle Chuck had fought in Vietnam, and I saw on his face a horrible familiarity with death. All of a sudden the room was too small, and closing in. Everyone wanted to reach me, or hug me, or "something" me. And all I wanted was to get out of there. I remember climbing over the back of a chair, past my Uncle Neil, and racing for the door.

Somehow I made it to my bedroom and lay down on the bed. My discipleship leaders and Beth came in. They sat there around me while I said nothing. After a few minutes I looked over at the clock on the night table, and the most relieving thought in the world overwhelmed me. It was just past midnight, and I said to them, "It's a new day."

November 3, 1998, was finally over.

Beth

The funeral was hard. Somewhere around 1,000 people came and that kind of support was a bit overwhelming. But Mom and I survived that week. I remember my school friends hanging out at my house that Wednesday and Thursday. They were constantly trying to be funny and make me smile. I remember Ryan Wilson and Jason Pippen going into my closet and putting on some of my girliest clothes. They came out and did a little drag show, and even I had to admit that they were hilarious.

When Friday rolled around, I decided to go back to school. My family thought I was crazy and said I should wait—I had stayed home only three days—but I knew I could not hide out forever, and I figured by going on Friday, I would have the whole weekend to recover. Every time I walked into a classroom that Friday I had a teacher stare dumbfounded at me. My physics teacher, who was one of my all-time favorite teachers, blurted out, "You have balls, April Jones. I can't believe it." He shook his head at me, and then when he realized what he had said, and where he had said it...well, that was actually kind of funny.

Of those days right after Dad died, my most vivid memory is of an afternoon about two weeks later. I came home from school, as usual, but instead of turning on the T.V. and assuming my zombie-like trance, I picked up a book I had seen at the funeral and at the house after. It was a book with pictures of my dad, and pages where people had signed and written things about him. I don't know what I was thinking, or if I was thinking, because reading what they had written was certain to turn out badly.

I started flipping pages and sporadically reading entries. The whole experience was almost surreal. Until this moment, I had retained remarkable composure. That inner strength I depended on so long had not yet abandoned me, and on the surface I looked like a coping-miracle. But that afternoon, somewhere in the middle of words written by my cousin Bryan, I remembered thinking oddly that the page looked blurry. Much too slowly, it dawned on me that maybe I was crying. I remember putting down the book and walking to my bathroom for a tissue. Suddenly I collapsed on the tile floor. There, alone, probably for two hours, I wept and rocked. Wept and rocked. The flood gates had finally been opened.

I promise you that I did not open them. Typical April would have never looked at that book. Without God's hand guiding me that day, I would have never done something so emotionally careless. But God, on the other hand, knew it was time to break me. He saw that it was time to make me see that my inner strength was not real, lasting strength at all. He was, and could be, my only lasting strength. He was ready and willing, and was just waiting on me to let go of the last threads of my composure. Why? So that He could begin stitching me back together. ...Stronger. Better. He knew how to do it so much better than I.

When I finally stopped crying and I realized what had happened, I pulled myself to my feet and called Beth. It was one of the shortest conversations in history.

"Hello?"

"It's me," I said.

"I'll be right over."

When she arrived, I was waiting at the door, armed with tissues, a pen, and some stationery with a long, red rose on it.

She asked only one question, "So where are we going?"

"To the cemetery."

She nodded and we left. When we got there she walked down with me for a while, and then when she felt like I could manage on my own, she left me to have some time to myself and went to wait by the car. I don't know what I wrote in that letter that day. I remember addressing it to my two Daddies in heaven. I think I told Dad that I loved him and that eventually I was going to be OK because God was with me. I told him I was so happy he wasn't hurting anymore and that I was jealous that he had finally met Jesus. I probably told him some silly teenage things; I don't remember them now. But when I was done—just a page—I folded the letter and left it at his grave.

I walked back to the car. I was finally empty. No more words; no more tears for that day. And it was good. Beth gave me a hug and drove me home.

* * * * * * *

These days, when I am home I visit another grave at that cemetery. Dad and his mother are buried on one side of the cemetery, and my dear friend Beth is buried on the other. I would tell you that whole story, in as much detail as I've told my Honey's and my father's, but I've thought better of it. For one, I think a reader can only take in so many chapters of sadness, and well, there may have already been too many. But mostly, I want Beth's parents to read this book someday. It is as much for them as anyone, and I simply don't want them to have to relive every detail of that nightmare. When grandparents and parents die it is horrible, it is wholly tragic. But when someone's child dies, it is so horrible it is barely fathomable.

For our purposes, all you need to know is that when we were 18 years old, in September of 2000, just after we had started college in different states, Beth had a brain aneurysm. She had surgery and went into a coma. Then she woke up for two wonderful weeks there in the fall, like always, taking it all with amazing grace. Putting everyone else's needs before her own, she let everyone know that she loved them and that they should regret nothing pertaining to her. Then after a second emergency surgery she never woke up. Her parents had to decide to pull the plug, and they finally did so over Christmas. They brought her home, and she died there with her family on Christmas day. Beth loved Christmas more than anyone, so as sad as it might seem, it was fitting for Beth and her family.

During those few months when Beth was sick, I noticed something different about myself. This time I forsook being strong. This time I wept openly. This time I let others hold me up. It was horribly painful yet redeeming to grieve that way. It was a much deeper strength to let God be the strong one.

I still miss Beth. I still miss Honey and Dad. They still visit me in my dreams, and I still cry when I allow myself to remember. That will never change. But I wouldn't want it to.

Poems

It's possible that my life is best told through the poems I wrote along the way. So as for some last things I need to say, I'm letting my poems do the telling.

This first one I read to my class at our high school baccalaureate service.

Knowing

If I only knew…
the color of my wings,
        I could change my view
        of cluttered earthly things,
        and duties that bound
        would have to let go,
        bewildered by the sound:
        of beating wings from my soul.

I might fall—
fall for the dreams of my heart
fall into light from my dark
fall from this shell I'm 'cased in

fall to a place I could begin
fall into right from earth's wrong
fall into time with my song
fall into life:
        if I only knew the color and sound of flight.

If I only knew…
how a rosebud decides,
        to slip from the dew
        and blossom out wide.
        How doubt stares in wonder
        at this rose among thorns,
        amazed that from under
        winter's mask she was born.

I might fall—
fall for the dreams of my heart
fall into light from my dark
fall from this shell I'm 'cased in
fall to a place I could begin
fall into right from earth's wrong
fall into time with my song
fall into life:
        if I only knew how a rosebud decides.

If I only knew…
a Father up above,
        what's lost He'd renew
        and bathe hurts in love.

And when the sky opened wide
and poured out the rain,
I'd have His wings to fly
and I could bloom without shame.

I might fall—
fall for the dreams of my heart
fall into light from my dark
fall from this shell I'm 'cased in
fall to a place I could begin
fall into right from earth's wrong
fall into time with my song
fall into life:
if I only knew the Father of Love and Light.

* * * * * * *

A Daddy's Love

At a crowded party people laugh and smile,
yet he can't help but stare:
As his little girl walks in the room,
with flowers in her hair.

She looks around, suddenly lost,
and her eyes well up with tears.
Then she finds her strength, calls out his name,
and magically he hears.

He picks her up, dries off her face,
and thanks God for this chance.
As he tilts her chin, he asks her softly,
"Princess, may we dance?"

She hung the moon and lit the stars
as far as he can tell,
and no one else could heal his heart so
well.

Her hand in his, fears disappear,
as she tells him all her dreams,
and he hopes he'll be as much as she
believes.

She's all grown up, but daddy's gone,
...and she feels all alone.
So she reaches in, for the only other
Name she's ever known.

As the tears fall down, she calls on God,
and He lets go of the rain.
As it washes off her face, she feels it
washing off the pain.

The wind's embrace picks up her heart,
and she thanks God for this chance:
To tilt her chin and hear Him softly,
"Princess, may we dance?"

He hung the moon and lit the stars
as far as she can tell,
and no one else could heal her heart so well.

Her hand in His, fears disappear,
as she tells Him all her dreams,
and she trusts that He alone can meet her
needs.

* * * * * * *

Her Beth

The way the wind blows,
she knew not much of ends;
she wasn't sure much of beginnings,
and so God lent her a friend.

To the world they were just waking
and they felt just like the leaves,
though winds might try to break them,
together, they found their strength.

Because holding hands in rain storms
and holding hands in shine,
they brought their hearts to Jesus
and gave their spirits away to time.

But time doesn't warn of its arrows,
and two roses learned that life has thorns.
Bleeding, they rushed back to their Maker,
and Love healed what winds had torn.

Three strands can't be broken
and God wove a perfect braid.
Time would try to steal hope,
but friends learn how to be brave.

They bloomed in Love's freedom
until the petals began to fall.
Time knocked unexpected;
dreams, she tried to save them all.

She never forgot their promise.
She wanted to smile on the rain.
The rope she knew bound their hearts,
not even death could cause a fray.

But time doesn't warm of its arrows,
and two roses learned that life has thorns.
Bleeding, they rushed back to their Maker,
and Love healed what winds had torn.

The way the wind blows,
she knew not much of ends;
she wasn't sure much of beginnings
—just the treasure of her friend.

The world her friend was leaving
she knew wouldn't let her go.
She'd hold on until heaven
bore the fullness of their hope.

They'd held hands in rainstorms,
they'd held hands in shine,
they'd brought their hearts to Jesus,
so they'd soar in heaven's time.

Where time has no arrows for hurting,
and roses grow in fields without thorns.
Singing, saints praise their Savior,
and Love gives no one need to mourn.

* * * * * * *

(a poem/a letter/a string of thoughts, ...this October 15, 2005)

God Knows Best

You would have been 53 today.
But where would you be?

Watching football?
Working in the yard?
Taking a drive—
just because—
you always liked to do that?

You would have been 53 today,
But what gifts would be yours?

A couple new shirts?
Some very thick biographies?
And a card that said something real—
that touched you—
if just for a second?

You would have been 53 today,
But would you be well?

No more tubes and pills?
No more tattoos from radiologists?
No more pain—

but was the physical pain—
the worst pain, that you felt?

But you are 46.
And doing now, more I hope
than you told me—you hoped—you could do.

Not just a servant in a heavenly mansion.
Not unnoticed and unknown.
Not just scrubbing the golden floors—
of those—
you thought deserved to tread them more
than you.

No, Dad, you are 46.
And you are a prince in a heavenly hall.
Seated with a King, enjoying a feast.
Singing praises you never knew here, with us.
And singing them out—
from a heart—
the King has made new.

You are 46.
And you are with your Gracious Father.
You are 46.
And you have the gifts of eternal love and eternal life.
You are 46.

And you are well.
"For the last shall be first, and the first shall be last."
And it is well with my soul, Daddy.
For, if you were 53, today,
would either of us have such peace as this peace?

I learned a while ago, that I'd rather He have you than only me.
And so I sing,
All praises to our King!
Halleluiah! Halleluiah!
To the Lord of all!

I miss you, Dad.
But I am willing to feel those things,
because I loved you, first.

Please, tell the King I thank Him.
And that I know—
that He knows—
what is best.

Yes, our God knows best.

* * * * * * *

Weak

Anxious?

Parts of me.

Tired?

The eyes and heart.

Hopeful?

The core of me…

when the other core of me remembers to remember

the deeper joy, the story of faithfulness.

And He says my weakness is good.

And where I'm fragile…

He says that He is there—and He is seen all the more.

Anxious?

How can I be, when I see Him there?

Yes, when I see Him.

Needy.

Oh help me see you.

Help me.

How acute the need can be.

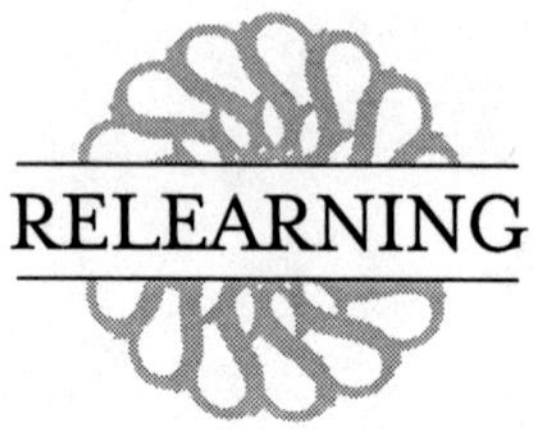

RELEARNING

Surrender

Fall 2005

It's strange.

I'm making everyday decisions, like "What am I going to have for lunch?" "What chips do I want with my turkey sub?" "What to drink—root beer or cream soda?" and then something happens. They don't have cream soda, and I'm angry. Alone in my car, familiar trees passing by the windows, and things are suddenly all wrong. I know where I want to be; I know who should be on the other end of my cell phone if not next to me in a lawn chair on the front porch. We'd have a cream soda. We'd watch a storm come in. "Daddy," I'd say, "I love him, Daddy. I'm not sure what I'm supposed to do right now, but I love him and that can make the rest more complicated. Sometimes it even makes it less important. Daddy, what do I do? Tell me where I'm wrong. Tell me what I'm thinking."

Dammit.

Dammit, Dad! I know there are tears back there, somewhere, and that pisses me off even more.

Brion, it's been one year since you came.

Dad, it's been seven years since you left. Why is love still so freaking hard to pin down?

Brion, I want a relationship with no problems, no

bumps, no heartache, but I know it doesn't exist. I just want to shake you—and hold you—and make you see me so closely and so fully. I want there to be absolutely nothing between us.

Dad, I wanted to shake you—I wanted you to hold me—I needed you to hug me and tell me it would all be OK. How did you see me so closely and so fully? Why is there so much of you in me? Because now you're not here, and I need to talk to you.

I could cry. I could break something. I could sit, exhale, and drink a cream soda. I just want a cold, smooth, comforting cream soda like the ones we drank during those summers out West. I just want everything to be OK and someone to tell me that it will be—and me to believe them. I've always wanted that.

I guess I have also always wanted love. But like my father I don't always comprehend what love could be. Damn you, cream soda. I didn't need this today. Oh, I don't know; maybe I did.

* * * * * * *

Right now I'd like to tell you that the lessons I've learned, once learned, were mastered forever. But they were not. Unconditional Love was the hardest thing for me to learn, trust, and comprehend that Thursday night in Mexico, June 22, 1995, when I was barely 13. And it is still the hardest thing.

Meeting and falling in love with Brion, who is now my husband, brought all my skepticism and distrust of love back to the surface. While I had never harbored anger toward God for the loved ones I had lost, suddenly I found myself petrified to love anyone else so deeply. I didn't want to lose anyone else. I didn't think I could bear it, but I was quickly learning that I couldn't bear to live without Brion either.

And so I began, once again, relearning Love and how to trust Love.

That's how it is. God is the greatest and most amazing unfailing Love there is, yet human memory is feeble and weak, and we must relearn His grace and love, over and over and over—the rest of our lives. Thankfully, He is a patient Teacher.

To illustrate this point, I began this book sometime in college shortly after Beth's death, and nearly seven years later, I am just finishing it. I began it, because I wanted to try to make sense of the things I had felt, to try to understand the parts of my father that were in me; to try and grasp the passion I had always feared but that I was beginning to realize ran through my veins. I began this book to remember and to understand Love. I also began it to communicate what little I knew about Love to others.

But why did it take me so long to finish? I suppose fear crept up again and made me put off writing the hardest parts. I didn't want to relive them on paper, so I hid them from myself and you. There again, I had much relearning to do. I had to remember to trust God to take me through it all again as I wrote. I had to relearn the lesson of faith. I had to relearn to trust Him in order to live out my own dream, my greatest passion: to write—and to tell this story before I told any others.

Unfortunately, Love is not the only lesson I must constantly relearn. I also have to relearn, over and over, that God both demands and deserves control over my life. When He broke my heart for the second time on my bathroom floor, He took control, and for a good while I let him have it. But then my human-ness eventually found a way to mess it up.

I say that the year Beth died is the year God taught me how to cry. But I still hate to do it. College was the time where I learned how to love God without the support group from home. But with all the pressures I now face in law school, I am relearning that one all over again, too. College was also a time of making mistakes and learning about forgiveness, but making mistakes and more fully understanding grace is not limited to college. It continues.

I must continue relearning many lessons. The trick is not to stop trying. It isn't hopeless. Hope is beautifully reborn and felt best when the lesson is fresh in your heart.

Breathing

(The fall of 2006: my last fall on the North Shore...just before Brion and I were married; just before we moved to Texas)

Mom called.

I was sitting on an open deck. Summertime twilight covered the tall trees that surrounded the yard—and me—wrapping around me like an oversized fall sweater. When my cell phone rang, a gigantic, bouncing standard poodle named Jackson was circling the catfish pond that is just below the deck. All was rosy, quaint, and peaceful. I was acting as a stand-in house-sitter for the night so that my roommate could catch a Red Sox game with her soon-to-be fiancé. Jackson lives in this house, with its beautiful oil paintings hanging on all the walls and the French country kitchen with built-ins to display white china. I like white china. I want white china.

Although I was sitting on the deck when the phone rang—mostly to giggle at Jackson—the adjacent screened-in porch is my favorite part of the house. I'm Greek when I'm in that room. It has tan wicker chairs puffed-up with white overstuffed cushions. The chairs surround a table covered in a pristine white table cloth which shows off the two large hurricane lamps at the center, each holding a tall island-blue candle. It's a wonderful room. Bigger because it's white, clean, and crisp. If only Mediterranean breezes could blow this far, then I'd know what it feels like to be in the Greek Isles.

In my imagination, I've already moved into this house. I've had several dinner parties here. I've served wonderful cheeses from the market and fresh vegetables from the organic farm just down the road. I've taken Jackson on long walks around the property, and chased him down when he gets distracted by birds. I've written wonderful poems and short reflections on my laptop when feeling Greek; when in my Greek room. And frequently those short respites have been interrupted by a close girlfriend stopping by to share a cup of coffee and good conversation out on my deck—or in my Greek room, if we're both feeling Greek for the moment. Yes, I like my life here; I like it very much.

But back to the phone call from Mom. She called to tell me that Mike's funeral is on Monday, and that Courtney is pregnant. Isn't that just like life? You're sitting idly one day, enjoying your fabulous imaginary life, and then something beautiful ends just while something else, also beautiful, is beginning. It's hard to grasp. I never know what is most appropriate in those moments. Do I pause to reflect the passing light, to honor and remember? Or do I let it pass while delighting in a budding light so new and virgin? I still don't know.

Mike is—was—Vicki's husband. Vicki, Courtney, and I grew up together and graduated high school the same year. We were in Girls' Discipleship together, and so that means that we exhaled life, together, on Sunday evenings, in someone's home, together, in a tight, safe, little circle God had made.

I didn't know Mike, but I know Vicki, and that is enough to make Mike's passing deeply felt. Mike loved Jesus, and so does his wife, and so I guess I'm comforted to know that she can handle this and that Mike's at peace. I know that she can handle this, simply because it has happened, and God does not allow us to hurt more than we can bear. But that makes me wonder—what was so strong within our small group of girls that we have been able to bear so much? Out of six of us, who grew within the walls of that small church, who lived within our mistakes and dreams, at 24 years old, five of us have experienced heartbreaking tragedy. Two of us have lost our fathers, two of us have lost husbands, and all of us have lost a dear friend, as one of us, Beth, is no longer living on this earth.

In the little circle that God made, what did He make so strong?

I know the answer. I feel the answer now. He never leaves, and He refuses to let that deserted feeling stick. Life has not fallen in the ways we all wanted, but God's love has never disappointed.

So tonight, writing this now in my Greek room, with the sunlight gone and crickets playing softly an unpublished symphony written by common grace, I must smile, remembering that joy is never far away. Courtney is pregnant. The circle that God made is opening up, and a new life is entering in. For that I must rejoice. Much like the New Life that met us there each Sunday evening when our souls practiced how to exhale, and He taught us how to, in turn, breathe in Life, this child is a true miracle.

Lord, as time has passed, we have needed our Sunday lessons. We have needed that foundation, and I am blessed to know that a little child will soon be some of the first fruits of the love You taught us. We will need that love continually. We will need our lessons in times to come. But right now it is Vicki's time. It is Vicki's time to remember how You once taught us to breathe.

So Lord, I pray now for her—please, just hold Vicki close. I pray for Brandy, Courtney, and Crystal—may they each hear Your voice in the morning and give over their day that is already Yours. And I thank You, Lord, for Beth.

For me? For me, I pray that I remember joy, faith, and love. Yes Lord, please, help me to have all of these—in a life of praise lifted up to You.

ENDINGS/BEGINNINGS

Finishing

Now I live in Texas. Brion and I are married, we have a dog-daughter named Austen, and I am starting my second year of law school. They tell me the next step is parenthood, and they may be right, but most days that's hard to imagine. Right now, more than anything, I simply want the words I have put down on paper here to have meaning in your life. I want you to find God's Love compelling. It is my sincere hope that my efforts here have somehow connected you to my very common story about a very uncommon Love.

As interviews for summer law clerkships approach, and dollar signs are mentioned or hinted at, I feel that same voice of practically calling, as it called to my father. In so many ways, that is why I had to finish this book. That is one of the many reasons I had to pen my story—and why I had to finish it now, in this season of my life. I know that some of my dreams may not bloom for a few more seasons, but I also know that I must keep trying. I know that I must trust God, because I also know that I have to make it to the trophy room for my father's sake.

I have to allow Love to win—and this time, not as the underdog.

Wish me more than luck. His <u>more</u> is what I wish for you.

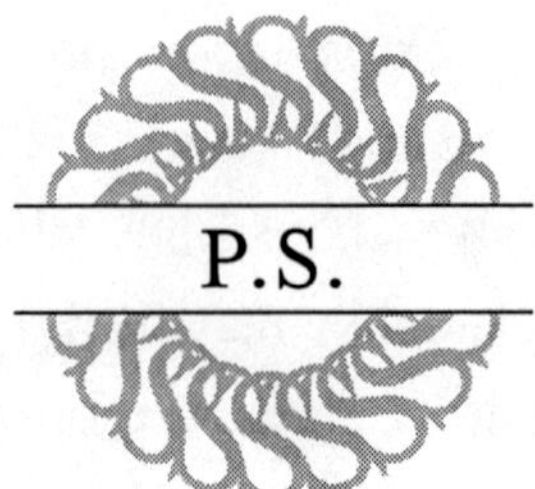

P.S.

New

The book is over, and I should leave all the rest of this stuff out of it. But if you're like me, sometimes you just want more. You want to know what happened next. You want to know the rest of the love story that was hinted at but not told. So I've included a little of Brion's and my story. Maybe a seasoned writer would say it is a bad idea, but oh well, this is my first book. I get to make these mistakes. And I've dared to do this because I think there is something beautifully redeeming in our story. The girl who needed love most, who feared love most, who desired love most—fell in love.

I wrote this letter to Brion the fall before we were married. We were engaged, and I was wading through the memories of past falls, as I always do that time of year, but this time I noticed some things were different. I wanted to express these discoveries to Brion as fully as I could, so I wrote him this letter.

September 24, 2006

Brion ~

My father was in my dreams two nights ago. It would be weird how dreams can bring back ghosts—so real and vivid—if it didn't happen, just like clockwork, every Fall. Then this morning in Church, the dream rushed over me, and I was back there, eight years ago, just for a moment. But then I saw you, in front of me on the stage, and I realized something was different. This has always been my life: memories of Fall always affect me, even if just in small ways, but I didn't have you in my life before. Brion we met in the Fall ...we fell in love in the Fall ...then the following Fall we realized we wanted to spend our lives together and by Christmas we were looking at rings. Then this year, on my birthday, you asked me to be your wife. Now this fall we are planning our wedding and our life together. And all of a sudden I realized that God had made my Fall new. I know you did not do this on purpose, but the fact that we got engaged on my birthday will from this day forward be a blessing I had never imagined. I always think of that horrible Fall actually beginning in the Summer, on my birthday. In so many ways it felt like I turned 16 and then our world fell apart. As it did this year, my birthday always falls on or around Father's day, and that year my birthday, along with Father's day, was the last family celebration we had with my Grandfather, my Dad and myself. Aug. 15th came, and Honey died. Then Oct. 15th came, and by then we all knew this was my father's last birthday. Then on Nov. 3rd he passed. Then two years later, as the memories were still so fresh and washing over me, Beth went into a coma in the Fall. Then about 2 months later, Fall finally ended when she died on Christmas. In so many ways, I have learned to hate the Fall, but today I've been thinking a lot about my time here on the North Shore, and I'm seeing a blessing I have until now missed. Leaves don't change in Florida.

Fall doesn't come alive at home, and it seems instead that a world that was once alive with Summer is suddenly dead and cold, without warning. Here, the transition is beautiful. Here I've made memories that seem more beautiful because of the colors of the leaves and the crispness of the air. Here I've learned to love Fall . . .as I've fallen in love with you. So anyway, I wrote a poem (part in church, and part this afternoon). It's actually not all that good—too simplistic—but I don't want to revise it; the simplicity of this blessing in disguise makes me happy.

You've made my Fall new
I see the leaves have color
I see their beauty falling
I need not wait for Spring
You've made my falling dancing
I used to follow daylight
And like it fade to sorrow
With Autumn memories
Now You've coaxed my heart to fall
To trust that light can linger
To linger in your gaze
To dance on fallen things
You've made my falling new
With hope the days get shorter
As I see love's beauty falling
Into memories writ like Spring

Happy

On January 13, 2007, Brion and I were married in the First Baptist Church of Eustis, Florida. It was the perfect wedding, and the perfect day. Since poetry had narrated so much of our relationship, as it has my life, I wrote a poem to Brion to be read on our wedding day. Brion's sister, Kristie, an excellent speaker, graciously agreed to read the poem during the ceremony. It was printed on the back of the programs, but Brion heard it for the first time the moment just after I made that breath-catching, purposeful, elated walk down the aisle to stand by his side. Kristie read the poem from a white journal which Karen Kelly, a dear family friend, had made for me the week after my father died. Karen knew I journaled much too much, so she made me something to have with me on my wedding day when my father couldn't be there. Although no one else at our wedding knew about the origins of the journal from which Kristie read, I did, and that gave me even more joy, faith, hope and love, on a day when I thought feeling any more of these things wasn't possible.

Such Love

deep breath
small steps.
can it be that this is real?
can one heart feel what I feel   for you
...such love

deep joy
fast pulse.
can they hear my heartbeat too?
can they believe that God made you   for me
...such love

deep hope
glad tears.
who taught you how to share my pain,
to shield the rain and bring the sun with just my name
from you
...such love

deep faith
long prayers.
I pray to give the love I've known,
out of the girl that love has grown   from me
...such love

deep love
big God.
how does He know just what we need?
How did He send His Son to die the King   for us
...such love

so...*deep breaths*
small steps.
hand in hand this road is new—
may we love, as He first loved...the love that's true
in us

...such LOVE.

An Afterward of Thanks

Mom: Thank you for loving me more than life and always believing that all my dreams really would come true. I could never have asked for more than that.

Dad: Thank you for imagination, passion, and for that hunger to always know more.

Honey: Thank you for instilling in me the desire to tell great stories and a desire to do all things with honor.

Beth: Thank you for friendship. Thank you for your goodness: your gentle, sweet spirit which I never had and always admired.

Vicki and Don Procia: Thank you for your daughter and your love.

Brian: Thank you for loving me—as He loves me—for wanting to know every part of me, and simply continuing to show me a selfless, enduring love I still do not understand. (And thank you for helping me finally finish this dream...with wine and bubbles, of course.)

Skipper and Chuck: Thank you for finding something in these pages that you wanted others to read—and making it happen. Thank you most for always keeping me in your heart.

Kristen: Thank you for never giving up on this story. Thank you for reading it and rereading it, and pushing me until I actually finished. It would not have happened without your tireless prodding.

Lolly: Thank you for guiding me and always identifying with and showing me the way out of my writing woes.

My family: Thank you for believing that blood is thicker than water and that family really is the most important thing. Thank you all for loving me despite all my stubborn faults and for loving my mom and my dad through It all.

My friends who walked beside me before, when I was sad, when I needed help and did not always allow you to give it: Thank you for not giving up on me.

My friends who walked beside me after, when you taught me to, little by little, trust happiness: Thank you for not giving up on me.

Trinity Evangelical Church of Eustis Florida: Thank you for introducing me to my Savior and making me a disciple.

Him: Thank you. ...for everything.

LaVergne, TN USA
21 December 2010
209715LV00001B/64/P